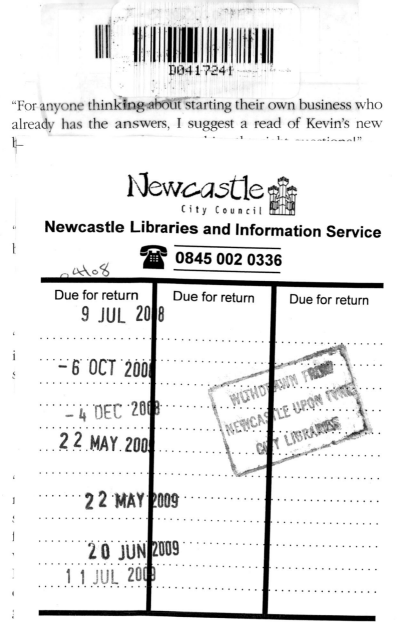
"For anyone thinking about starting their own business who already has the answers, I suggest a read of Kevin's new

Newcastle
City Council

Newcastle Libraries and Information Service

☎ **0845 002 0336**

Graham Clayworth,
International Liaison Partner, BDO Stoy Hayward

"Kevin has approached a topic every aspiring entrepreneur should read. I would pass a law that made all legal and financial advisers obliged to provide this book to people starting a business for the first time. There is no better business experience than starting, building and running one's own enterprise but as Kevin's book demonstrates, it isn't for the faint-hearted."

Paul Simons,
Founder, Cagney and former CEO, Ogilvy

Start

Start

How to get your business underway

Kevin Duncan

Includes hundreds of brilliant pieces of advice from those who have been through the pain and pleasure of starting their own business

CAPSTONE
be inspired!

John Wiley & Sons, Ltd

Other Wiley Editorial Offices

John Wiley and Sons Inc., 111 River Street, Hoboken, NJ 07030, USA

Jossey-Bass, 989 Market Street, San Francisco, CA 94103-1741, USA

Wiley-VCH Verlag GmbH, Boschstr. 12, D-69469 Weinheim, Germany

John Wiley and Sons Australia Ltd, 42 McDougall Street, Milton, Queensland 4064, Australia

John Wiley and Sons (Asia) Pte Ltd, 2 Clementi Loop #02-01, Jin Xing Distripark, Singapore
129809

John Wiley & Sons Canada Ltd, 6045 Freemont Blvd, Mississauga, ONT, L5R 4J3, Canada

Wiley also publishes its books in a variety of electronic formats. Some content that appears
in print may not be available in electronic books.

Anniversary Logo Design: Richard J. Pacifico

Library of Congress Cataloging-in-Publication Data

Duncan, Kevin, 1961-
  Start : how to get your business underway / Kevin Duncan.
      p. cm.
  Includes index.
  ISBN 978-1-84112-794-1 (pbk. : alk. paper)
  1. New business enterprises.   2. Entrepreneurship.   I. Title.
    HD62.5.D877 2007
    658.1'1--dc22   2007050367

Typeset in 11.5/14 pt ITC Garamond by Thomson Digital
Printed and Bound in Great Britain by TJ International Ltd, Padstow, Cornwall, UK

Substantial discounts on bulk quantities of Capstone Books are available to corporations,
professional associations and other organizations. For details telephone John Wiley & Sons
on (+44) 1243-770441, fax (+44) 1243 770571 or email corporatedevelopment@wiley.co.uk

"We have no money so we will have to think."

Lord Rutherford

This book is dedicated to my mum; my wonderful daughters Rosanna and Shaunagh; and my brilliant partner Sarah Taylor.
As predicted, the Sleeping Lion awoke.

In memory of my father James Grant Duncan, 1923–1989.

ACKNOWLEDGEMENTS

Once again, big respect to Gray Jolliffe for the superb cartoons, and to Sam for the introduction.

Thanks to all my mates for all their advice and support: Simon Docherty, Mark Earls, Tina Fegent, Mark Gordon, John Hamilton-Hunt, Dave Hart, Rassami Hok-Ljungberg, Daf Jones, Mark Joy, Graeme Leno, Nic Ljungberg, Jim Marshall, John Owrid, Melanie Ryder, Paul Speers, Glyn Taylor; all the gang at Turner Duckworth, especially Moira and Bruce; and the team at Prontaprint Victoria.

And for reading an early version: Robert Ashton, Graham Clayworth, Ian Mason, Shaun Orpen and Paul Simons.

For the introduction to James Murray Wells: David Magliano.

A big thank you too to my team at Capstone, particularly to John Moseley for believing in my stuff.

Thanks go to all those who took the trouble to answer my questions: Robert Ashton, Steve Barber, Renee Botham, Sue Buckle, Andrew Butcher, Paula Carter, Will Collin, Chris Cowpe, Vanessa Dalton, Peter Dann, Peter Davies, Matthew Durdy, Tim Ellis, Anne Esler, Ian Fairbrother, Ian Farrow, Tina Fegent, Marcel Feigel, Paul Flynn, Giles Fraser, Peter Gaze, Sheila Gimson, Laurence Green, Steve Greensted, Irma Hamilton-Hunt, John Hartley, Gordon Haxton, Tom Helliwell, Rassami Hok Ljungberg, Camilla Honey, Ian Humphreys, Julian Hurst, Vanella Jackson, Chris Jenkins, Sarah Jennings, Cathy Johnson, Daf Jones, Caroline Kinsey,

Stephen Knight, Peter Law, Stephen Martin, Zena Martin, Simon Mathews, Chris Matthews, Mark McCallum, Peter McCamley, Manisha Mehta, Juan Montes, Adam Morgan, Ivan Mulcahy, Griselda Mussett, Mo Murphy, Michael Pagan, Graham Rittener, Ben Robbins, Julian Saunders, Andrew Sawkins, Paul Simons, Paul Speers, Sarah Taylor, Andy Tilley, David Turner and Richard Wyatt-Haines.

If you ever need any inspiration, or proof that we all go through the same troubles, read their words of wisdom and you'll feel much better.

And finally many thanks to the good people at *The Week Magazine* ("All you need to know about everything that matters") – the source of the majority of the quotations in this book.

ABOUT THE AUTHOR

Kevin Duncan worked in advertising and direct marketing for twenty years. For the last eight years he has worked on his own as a business adviser, marketing expert and author. He teaches at Canterbury University, and advises various businesses as a non-executive director, business strategist and trainer.

He has two daughters, Rosanna and Shaunagh, and lives in Westminster. In his spare time he travels to strange parts of the world, releases rock albums and flies birds of prey.

Also by Kevin Duncan:
Teach Yourself Running Your Own Business
Teach Yourself Growing Your Business
So What?

If you want to be alerted to future books by the author, or want to contact him:
kevinduncan@expertadvice.co.uk
expertadviceonline.com
kevinduncan.typepad.com

CONTENTS

Introduction

Thanks for picking up this book. You are obviously in the mood for change, and you have already admitted to yourself that you might need a bit of help. That's two massive steps already. People set up businesses when they get fed up with the way other companies do things, or if they have a brilliant idea, or if they get booted out of their corporation and have no choice (there's no embarrassment with this any more – it happened to me on several occasions).

There must be millions of books about starting your own business, so why should this one be any different? Well, part of it may lie in what this book does *not* cover. Firstly, it is not a self-help book that takes you step by step through all the technical stuff such as how to do your tax return or visit the bank for a loan. There are plenty of other books that do this. Secondly, it is not my life story from rags to riches. These can be interesting, but more often than not they are very predictable. You know the sort of stuff: I started off in my front room, then we had to work in the garage, then we had to borrow some money from my uncle, and so on. Unless these stories have a fascinating angle that is directly relevant to your situation, then they may not help you, the ordinary person, to cope with what you are going to go through.

No, what I am interested in is how you *feel*.

I have long held the belief that you cannot run your own business successfully if you haven't got your head straight when you are off duty. As a sole trader, your home and work life are often indivisible. You need to be balanced and calm in both areas otherwise you will self-destruct.

That's what this book is all about: how to set up your own business, run it successfully, and stay sane. Easier said than done? It can be done, believe me. All you need is good advice, the desire to learn, an inquiring mind, and a sense of humour. That's why I have interviewed so many people for this book – so that you can see that they all went through exactly the same stuff as you, and to let you know that it absolutely can be done.

Dive in and enjoy the journey.

Starting from Scratch

This chapter covers many of the reasons for starting a business. Ignore everyone else, what do you want to do? What are you really passionate about in life? Going to work could be like going to play if you choose the right line of work. Questions you have to address include: what exactly is the idea, what will your business be, why do your customers need you, and will your idea make money? A poor plan, even if brilliantly executed, is still a poor plan. Are you in the mood for change?

Ignore everyone else, what do *you* want to do?

Starting from scratch is a scary thing. Here I sit in front of an empty desk with a book to write. It's the second of January and you have no business, no customers, and no tangible manifestation of your brilliant idea. Don't panic. A lot of us have been there. You are not alone. Put the kettle on – we've got some serious thinking to do.

> *"The greatest pleasure in life is doing what people say you cannot do."*
>
> **Walter Bagehot**

Frankly, when it comes to the matter of starting your own business, for once we are not remotely interested in anyone else's opinion. Ignore everyone else. What do *you* want to do? Don't rush the answer. If you do, you may well end up doing something that is less than satisfying. No, go for the thing that you really fancy. Don't worry at this stage about how you are going to do it. Just focus on the main point, and keep looking at it until you are satisfied that it is right for you.

This book is all about you and your aspirations, and to help navigate you through how to realize them, I have asked lots of other people what they went through and why they bothered. The full survey is in Appendix II, so you can go into more detail if a particular story fascinates you, but I have drawn out the main themes as we go along so we can learn from others and confirm that everyone goes through what you will.

Reasons for starting a business

So let's begin by looking at why people bother to go to all the trouble of starting their own business in the first place. In the survey I asked five questions. The first was *What made you start your business?* Over sixty people answered, so we have quite a decent spread of opinion to work with. The range of reasons for starting a business is fascinating:

- I hated my boss.
- Couldn't stand the politics.
- Frustration with current job.
- Got fired or made redundant.
- Convinced there must be a better way.
- Wanted to be my own boss/have more control.
- The chance to use my brain for my own benefit.
- Run my life as I want.
- Life changes everything.
- Wanted to take a risk.
- Always wanted to.
- Wanted the challenge.
- Wanted to create my own dream job.
- Spotted an opportunity.
- Had a safety net.
- Wanted to make a lot of money.
- A combination of fear and ambition.

I should stress that this is not a quantitative survey, so there is no particular order or bias to the answers. Let's work through them to see what we can learn, and so that you can work out what your own reasons are.

I hated my boss

Shocking, but true. Many people cite as their main reason for setting up a business the fact that they couldn't stand their boss. Some bosses are undoubtedly incompetent, but the comment mainly seems to refer to their unacceptable behaviour – boorish approaches, bullying, sexism, arrogance, a despotic, dominating style – you name it. No matter what corporations do to prevent this appalling activity, some bad apples always seem to slip through the net. No one should have to put up with this sort of behaviour, and many don't. How about you? To see how this sort of approach from inappropriate bosses can spur someone on to start their business, take at look at the story of Julian Saunders:

"What motivated me to start my own business was a desire for freedom from corporate life, prompted by the truly loathsome experience of working under my previous boss. It confirmed what I already knew in my heart of hearts. I could not put up with all the nonsense of big ad agencies any more. I had grown out of it."

Julian's full story is in Appendix II. Recognize any symptoms from your current job?

Couldn't stand the politics

This is not the same as hating your boss or being subjected to unreasonable working practices. Political companies foster an atmosphere in which people do not say what they mean. Or they don't mean what they say. Either way, if you value your honesty and integrity (see Chapter 5), then you won't be able to tolerate this type of environment for very long. In my experience, there are two main things that happen when an individual can't stand a political environment.

1. You don't say what you mean and end up hating yourself.
2. You say what you mean and eventually get fired.

If it's the first, then you may be in the right frame of mind to set up your own business. If it's the second, then read on, we've all been there.

Frustration with current job

You might not hate your boss and you might not work in a particularly political company, but you might still find large chunks of it deeply frustrating. The question is: to what extent? Mild, occasional frustrations may be natural and tolerable. Deep-seated and near-permanent frustration may mean it is time to move on. Millions have, and just think how much happier you could be.

Got fired or made redundant

I was made redundant three times in the 1990s. I was variously described as "surplus to requirements", "culturally incompatible" and "a mistake". It's charming, isn't it? And here I am offering my advice to the world! If my former employers were right, you had better stop reading now. Seriously though, there is no stigma any more to being chucked out by companies. It is even possible that the people who got rid of you may well since have suffered the same indignity themselves. So don't beat yourself up. If you want confirmation that millions have been in the same boat, read some of the experiences in Appendix II. Then take a deep breath and set about designing a much more rewarding life for yourself.

I am, or I became, unemployable

How brilliant is this? Many of our respondents have reached the conclusion that they simply aren't employable any more. Musicians and artists in particular will argue that they could never, ever "work for the man". Tim Ellis, a musician, writer and producer, says simply:

"I'm unemployable."

These types of people never even try normal employment. They just know that they would tell their boss where to stick it by lunchtime on the first day. I have massive admiration for this approach. These people really know what they stand for, and that is one of the most important parts of satisfaction in life and one's overall self-esteem.

Others, like me, seem to turn feral over the years, like cats that wander around our industrial parks and wasteland. Don't worry if this sounds like you. It's quite normal. As Paul Simons says:

"I believe that anyone who has created their own business successfully becomes unemployable."

As the years roll by, and as you experience the working practices of more and more companies, you will find yourself increasingly shaking your head and muttering to yourself: *"This is nuts."* If so, it may be time to make your move.

Convinced there must be a better way

If you think that the way your company is doing things is daft, then it's usually a short step to knowing what a better way is. Many who set up on their own are absolutely convinced that there is one. They know that the old way doesn't make sense and they can't stand it any longer. A bit of thought, a more flexible attitude, and the right approach from the start are all it needs to get underway. Is this you?

Wanted to be my own boss or have more control

Boss haters are often spurred to crave their own autonomy, but at a much milder level, a simple yearning for a higher degree of control is sometimes enough to push people over the edge. A lot of what people get asked to do in companies is hard for the individual to justify. For an extreme view of this phenomenon, read *Hello Laziness* by Corinne Maier (there is a summary in Appendix I). She goes so far as to assert that salaried work is the new slavery, and that the ideology of most businesses is no better than communism. A bit over the top perhaps, but the idea of being your own boss can be very appealing, especially if your current job involves doing all sorts of things for which there appears to be no decent reason.

The chance to use my brain for my own benefit

There is a close link between being the master of your own destiny and using your skills or brainpower for your own benefit. How frustrating it must be for intelligent people to find that their brains are not properly utilized. Or that their ideas and efforts are not harnessed by their employer in a fruitful way. It can be massively frustrating, and that is why so many people set up their own business.

> *"If I had only known... I would have been a locksmith."*
>
> **Albert Einstein**

Run my life as I want

Control, using your brain properly, running your life as you want. It all starts to come together as one thing. Those who hanker after these things have had enough of routine. The daily commute. The rigid working hours that bear no relation to the ebb and flow of the tasks that need doing. They all start to seem irrelevant. Flexible working has certainly helped a little. Some can do a proportion of their work from home. But still the corporate treadmill and millstone is there. Simple things such as the school run or waiting in for the gas man pale into insignificance when you run your own business. You can organize it all as you want it, and, to be honest, what grown-up, sentient being wouldn't want to do that?

Life changes everything

Moments in life can also be the trigger that fires the self-employed gun. Many women specify pregnancy as a fundamental reason why they stopped working for corporations. They simply use it as a neat way to bookend their conventional career and move onto something more fulfilling and flexible. Sometimes that means providing a mini version of what they originally did for the company. Other times, it's a complete relaunch in a totally new field. Lots of parents also set up their own businesses because they want to see their children grow up. The majority of these used to be women, but now many men do it too.

> *"A lot of businesses are being started by women who have been working for idiots for years. They know they can do their boss's job, but they know they will never be given it."*
>
> **Jean Denton, director of British Nuclear Fuels, 1988**

Wanted to take a risk

Look at the testimony from Andy Tilley:

"Reaching forty, being totally frustrated by the way my employer treated our discipline, ignored counsel and refused to change the structure of the business to adapt to the new landscape. At the same time hearing a story from a close friend who had attended Harvard. During a series of interviews with 75 men over 75, almost 80% said they wished they had taken more risks... Had to do it particularly as a number of my clients suggested it and said they would support it."

So 80% of men over 75 years old said they wished they had taken more risks. It was their biggest regret. Andy didn't want to be lying in a hospital bed as an old man wondering "*What if?*" So he got off his backside and got down to designing his version of what a business should be.

Always wanted to

For some, the desire to run their own thing often comes as a sort of epiphany, or as a result of the types of frustrations we have been looking at. But there are others who have always wanted to. Many are the sons and daughters of self-employed parents. Look at the cases of John Hartley and David Turner:

"In the end it's not a choice. It's a compulsion. I'm the only child of two self-employed parents so I grew up with it round the dinner table. I just didn't value corporate jobs. 'Real' work meant being self-employed, not being a salary man. That was the apprenticeship – learning a trade."

"My Dad had done it and preached its benefits. Also, I always liked making my own decisions."

They have seen at first hand how it works, and when they experience the madness of company life, the contrast is all the more stark. As Tom Helliwell says:

"I wanted to run my own business from the age of 15. I have some narcissistic traits which means I often believe I know more than my boss, and often my boss sees me as a threat, so I always used to get fired."

Wanted the challenge

Some crave the challenge of running their own business from a young age. They always wanted to. But others find it creeping up on them. It can strike at any time. Some become bored doing the same old thing, with the same old (lack of) results. They need a new challenge. Others trawl around scores of jobs and just can't find any stimulation, and that's one thing you are never short of when you run your own business.

Wanted to create my own dream job

Dreaming is another regular feature of setting up on your own. If you can design the job yourself, then why not make it your dream job? Sure, there will be some grim stuff to do, but if it's all for a cause that you invented or believe in, then somehow it all seems so much more worthwhile. The simple act of licking a stamp and putting it on an envelope can take on a whole new meaning when it contains one of your own invoices.

Spotted an opportunity

There are some who simply say that they saw an opportunity and went for it. In this respect, it doesn't really matter what their circumstances were before they made the leap. They may have been running another business, or they may have been working for someone else. The point is, they had an idea, and then had the courage of their convictions to get on and do it. This will be a recurring theme in the book, but if you want to think more about that now, then go straight to Chapter 4.

Had a safety net

A few people are honest enough to admit that they had the benefit of a safety net when they set up their business. This certainly helps to reduce stress levels, although in some cases there are those who think it also makes people too comfortable and reduces their drive. The nature of the safety net varies hugely. Sometimes it is a significant redundancy payment. Perhaps a continuing contract of some kind with your former employer as a consultant. Others have husbands, wives or partners who earn and are prepared to support the household until the new business is fully underway. It's a magnanimous gesture and it happens frequently. And finally there are those incredibly lucky people who have independent means, or, put another way, are loaded and so can have a dabble. If you are one of these people, then I don't think this book is for you – you have to really need your business to work to be interested in the day-to-day minutiae that preoccupy the average sole trader.

Wanted to make a lot of money

Funnily enough, this is one of the least common reasons cited for starting a business. A few do, but far more say that you shouldn't do it for the money, but to enable yourself to do something you love. The money comes later. A fine balance, some would argue. For an exploration of the philosophy behind this, have a look at Chapter 10 and see what you believe.

A combination of fear and ambition

Some people are candid enough to cite fear or ambition as their reason for starting their business. Have a look at what Paul Simons says:

"In truth, a combination of fear and ambition. The fear was becoming a highly paid 40 something with my life held in someone else's hands, on a whim. Very scary. On the ambition front, I believed there was a better way!"

The fear seems to creep in as people get older – they don't want to spend their entire life in the thrall of someone else, and they don't want to end their days thinking *"If only…* Ambition takes all sorts of forms. Even those who have been the chief executive of a huge corporation can have the ambition to do their own thing.

What are you really passionate about in life?

Much of it boils down to what you feel passionate about. If you are very lucky, you may be able to turn a passion or hobby into an income-generating business. If this is a true passion like music or sport, then the fit can be utterly brilliant. But more likely it will be some sort of subsidiary talent that you used to pursue in your youth or that you currently squeeze into what little spare time you have. What side interest do you have that could form the basis of your own business?

How going to work could be like going to play

Those who manage to crack this problem end up saying that going to work is effectively like going to play. It just doesn't feel like work in the sense that we understand it in corporations. This may in large part be down to the enjoyment of the subject, and your intrinsic interest in it, but it is also helped by lots of little things that make life more palatable: the lack of a commute, more relaxed clothing, flexible working hours, greater holiday freedom, a better link between effort and reward, and much more. We will cover lots of these in the book.

What exactly is the idea?

So now let's get down to the small matter of deciding what your business is going to be. In a sense, this is an odd thing for a book to get into: I couldn't possibly tell you what to do without knowing all about you. But what I can do is offer up lots of questions that will help you to sort out your thinking. Let's have a look at some of the questions that have been really useful for my clients and students.

What will your business be?

Have a look at Figure 1.1 and work your way through the questions. Don't panic if you can't answer them in full – just do your best at this stage. We will get much more precise about it in the next chapter.

- What are you going to sell?
- What product(s) or service(s)?
- At what price(s)?
- Who will buy them?
- How many people will buy them, and how often?
- What is the cost of sale? (Production, marketing, rent, staff costs, etc.)
- What is the margin?
- Is that viable?
- So will you do it then?

Fig. 1.1: What will your business be?

What are you going to sell? Here you need to define your approximate product or service, such as cleaning services, plumbing, babysitting, language translation services, whatever. Then get more specific: what product(s), precisely, are you offering? List them all out with descriptions as clearly as possible. At what price(s)? Now attach a price to each one. If you don't know yet, then guess.

Now think about who will buy your products or services. You don't need to get into complicated target audience definitions. Stick to simple labels such as age, sex, income level, geographical location and social circumstances. For example, to what age band will your product appeal? Is your product relatively cheap or expensive? Is it universal or exclusive? Can it be purchased from far away or is it very much a local offering? Is your product bulky? This may determine ease of purchase and help to define your likely catchment area. By answering these types of questions you can break potential audiences down into small categories and estimate their likelihood of purchasing your product. Then you can add up the rough number of purchases you hope to get in a year.

Your approximate picture of the shape of the business is building. By sketching out the price, product and likely number of purchases you will have a total sales figure emerging. Now you need to estimate the cost of sale. That's all the stuff that it costs you to provide the product or service: the cost of production, distribution, marketing, rent, staff costs, and so on.

Subtract the costs from the anticipated sales figure, and what is left is the margin or profit. Don't worry about minute detail at the moment. We are simply knocking up a quick ready reckoner to see whether your business idea is viable or not.

Stare at the figures for a moment and ask yourself: is that viable? If it is, then you may be onto something (you can be specific about the true figures later). If it isn't, then try to work out why. Is it a fundamental flaw, or a small tweak? Dig around to establish the reason, and don't mislead yourself. If it's flawed, then it's flawed and you need a new idea. Never start a business on a false premise, otherwise you will lose your money and your livelihood. For the moment, this exercise allows you to address the basic question: so will you do it then?

Why do they need you?

The simple exercise we have just done usually works for businesses that have a particular product or thing to sell. But it may need further elaboration if you are proposing to base your business on a service or a new idea. If that is the case, then try the lines of inquiry in Figure 1.2.

Start by articulating what expertise you are offering. This sounds straightforward enough, but my clients and students have terrible trouble doing it. You are not allowed to launch into a 10-minute diatribe riddled with acronyms and jargon. Tell it straight so any layperson can understand it.

- What expertise are you offering?
- Does the customer know what they want?
- If not, can you guide their choice appropriately?
- What do they stand to gain or lose from using you?
- Are there any other considerations?
- If so, clarify why.

Fig. 1.2: Why do they need you?

> *"The first step to getting the things you want out of life is this: decide what you want."*
>
> **Ben Stein, quoted in the Fort Lauderdale Sun-Sentinel**

The next crucial question is: does the customer know what they want? This sounds a bit daft, but on investigation you will find that it applies to hundreds of markets, particularly when you are selling advice. If you go to a lawyer, you may know what your problem is, but you need the expert to explain what you need to fix it. It's the same with information technology. So ask yourself if your customer knows what they want, and find a way of describing it that helps to support why they need you, and why they should pay your prices for what you have to offer.

If not, your offer should be orientated around guiding their choice appropriately. You need to explain what they stand to gain or lose from using you, and what the best solution is. Then ask yourself whether there are any other considerations that either they or you won't have thought of and, if so, clarify why and how they affect things. When you have raked through all of this, live with it for a while and ask yourself the killer question:

Will that make money?

If the answer is no, not really, then you may need to rip it up and start again. I should point out at this stage that I am not an advocate of rampant greed. If the business isn't going to make a reasonable profit then you probably won't be satisfied with it. In a few exceptional circumstances, you may conclude that it is fine that the business does not make money. Not-for-profit organizations, charities and second businesses that are hobbies spring to mind.

More likely though, you will indeed want your business to make money. Quite how much is up to you. One person's fortune is another's loose change. Just make sure that the effort put in appears to be a fair trade for the income derived. If you design a model now that already shows that you will be rushing around like a fly in a bottle just to make a few quid a year, then redesign it now. There's no point in generating a poor plan, only to execute it brilliantly.

Poor plan, brilliantly executed

You'd be amazed how many people have a poor plan for their business. If they were genuinely unaware of this at the start, then you could just about forgive them for reaching the end of the first year and expressing dismay and surprise at the fact that they haven't made a bean. Bizarrely though, many people go ahead and launch their business even though they already know the plan is bad. *"Ah yes, that was always a slight flaw, but I needed to convince the bank manager"* is a common comment. On no account let this be you. In my previous book *So What?* I referred to the acronym RIRO, the "Rubbish in, rubbish out" principle that computer experts use to describe poor data in their programming equations, and it's the same thing here. A poor plan will lead to a poor business performance, so don't start with one. Now is your once-only chance to get it right.

Some things to consider

Now ponder on these twelve points

1. If your business is going to operate in a specific area, will the market support it?

2. For example, if you plan to open a restaurant, how many already exist, what type of service do they offer and what are their prices like?

3. How do they position themselves – greasy spoon, haute cuisine or take away?

4. Will the area support another restaurant or is it already saturated?

5. Check out rival prices and position your product accordingly.

6. What kind of people will buy your product?

7. What will your (best) customers tend to have in common?

8. Can you reach all of your customers through the same communication channels?

9. Do your potential customers fall into different groups?

10. Are there different buying circumstances, for example: planned, impulse or special occasion?

11. How often will you communicate with your customers?

12. Have I thought of a decent name for my business?

What's in a name?

This is a matter of personal taste, but I think it is really worth dreaming up a distinctive, memorable name for your business. There are five main types of company name:

1. Descriptive (*Premier Sandwiches*).
2. Owner-named (*Dave's Sandwiches*).
3. Multiple owner-named (*Johnson Hobson Wilson Potato Peeler*).
4. Pointless initials (*DS Ltd*).
5. Irrelevant but memorable (*Orange,* as in the mobile phone company).

If you wish to portray a solid but unremarkable image, then the descriptive approach may be justified. I would stress, however, that inventive branding has permeated almost every product category these days, so you should be as brave as you can be.

The second option may be relevant if you have a reputation from a past life and it will be helpful for past clients to know that it's your business. In the case of *Dave's Sandwiches,* this is unlikely, but if you are a prominent expert in a specific field, then it may be relevant. Multiple owner-named company names are grim, and the size of the name usually reflects the massive egos of the partners. Lawyers and advertising agencies are famous for this type of thing. Classic examples include:

Abbott Mead Vickers BBDO
Boase Massimi Pollitt Doyle Dane Bernbach
Rainey Kelly Campbell Roalfe/Young and Rubicam
Bygraves Bushell Valladares Sheldon
Still Price Court Twivy D'Souza

And the truly outstanding *Messner Vetere Berger McNamee Schmetterer.* Really, you couldn't make this stuff up. Can you imagine what it would be like to be working on the switchboard at that company? Resist this route if you possibly can: it usually just leads to hoots of derision from potential customers.

Option four, pointless initials, is also highly undesirable. A quick glance at the phone book reveals thousands and thousands of these acronyms. Initials say nothing about you and are unremarkable. Try to resist using them.

The last option, irrelevant but memorable, can be fun if it is done well. For example, if you work in a fairly dry sector, the use of a fun, lively name might soup it up a bit. How about funeral directors called *Wakey Wakey?* Or an estate agent called *Sharks?* Less controversially perhaps, accountants called *Gherkin* would be more memorable than *Dawkins, Brown and Reaper.* Years ago I was told of some solicitors called *Mann Rogers and Greaves*, which sounded like a pretty good summary of the human condition. And more recently my friend Graham Clayworth tells me there are estate agents called *Doolittle and Dalley*, which is quite superb.

Now here are my personal favourites (as you'll see, I can't resist a pun):

Baguette Me Not (sandwich shop)
Bare Necessity (tanning salon)
Bloom in Waterloo (florist)
Deb 'n' Hair (hairdresser)
Ice Pics (film production)
Pollen Nation (florist)
Pure Waffle (coffee shop)
Rhubarb (public relations)
The FulHam Sandwich (sandwich shop in Fulham)

I think the florists and sandwich shops have it right.

Guts, heart or head?

People talk about having a gut reaction. I don't know about you, but I would not base any decision on an internal organ whose purpose is purely digestive. Hearts are pretty useless too. Sure, they keep you alive by pumping blood around, but that doesn't make them much cop at deciding whether your business is a goer or not. No, when it comes to making this decision, use your head.

> *"Carl Sagan was proud to be agnostic when asked whether there was life elsewhere in the universe. When he refused to commit himself, his interlocutor pressed him for a 'gut feeling' and he immortally replied: 'But I try not to think with my gut. Really, it's okay to reserve judgement until the evidence is in'."*
>
> **From The God Delusion by Richard Dawkins**

In the mood for change?

Right, so we have covered a number of the preliminary considerations when you are starting a business from scratch. You should have ignored everybody else and worked out what *you* want to do. If it helps, use the springboard of one of the emotions we discussed to provide the energy and impetus for your new idea – the frustrations with your previous job, your desire for autonomy, your eye for an opportunity – whatever spurs you on.

Then you'll have concentrated on precisely what the idea is, and done a rough calculation as to whether it will make you money. Other considerations such as the construction of your likely customer base, the realism of your plan and the name of your company should be beginning to gel. If you still think you are miles off, review the checklist and go round again if necessary. If you think you have a rough shape, then you are ready for Chapter 2.

> *"Change before you have to."*
>
> **Jack Welch**

Chapter 1 checklist

1. Ignore everyone else and decide what *you* want to do.
2. Try to base this on something you are really passionate about.
3. Decide exactly what the idea is.
4. Articulate precisely what your business will be.
5. Work out why your potential customers need you.
6. Will that make money?
7. If your plan is poor, change it.
8. Choose a distinctive, memorable name.
9. Use your head and keep the emotion out of it.
10. Brace yourself for change.

Pecked to Death
by Ducks

2

This chapter explains why the rough shape will do. We are looking for progress not perfection. The one-page business plan enables you to plan your business in six steps. How much money do you really want? What's the proposition? Can you describe it to your mum? Should it be big or bold? Might small be better than big? So is it a goer then?

Why the rough shape will do

There are many schools of thought when it comes to planning your business. You will probably have gathered by now that I come from the "keep it brief" school. To a large extent, the work you have just done in the first chapter should reveal whether your business idea has a decent chance of working or not. You don't need to be a master mathematician to get a broad feel for things. All you need after the figures exercise is some basic honesty and common sense. If it doesn't make sense, then think harder until it does. If the numbers don't add up, keep changing things round until they do. Then if they still don't, you may have to face facts and move on to a new idea.

The rough shape will do. Don't get too detailed unless you are forced to do so by some potential backer, but even then, tell them that you are looking at the big picture, not the minutiae. This chapter will add some detail to the rough plan you knocked up in the last one, but not so that the whole thing is pecked to death by ducks. Death by a thousand cuts is no way to start a business. Each small withdrawal from the original idea may not seem too outrageous, but eventually they can often add up to a serious erosion of what was originally very exciting. We are concerned with preserving the central idea (assuming it is sound in the first place), and we want to keep it as pure as possible. The diluted version that has been got at by hundreds of advisers and consultants will usually be significantly poorer, so don't let that happen. Remember, it's your business, not theirs.

Envelopes, fag packets and postcards

Some of the best business plans in the world are scribbled on whatever is available at the time. The back of an envelope, a cigarette pack or a postcard will do. In his book *How Not To Come Second*, David Kean raises the idea of a pitch on a postcard. The basic idea is a good one – if you can't fit your argument on one, then it's too complicated. There is a summary in Appendix I. The problem with a lot of ideas these days is that they are just too long-winded. Frankly, if a layperson can't get the gist of it in one sentence, then it is unlikely to have sufficient appeal to be a financial success.

> *"Solitude is the school of genius."*
>
> **Edward Gibbon, quoted in The Guardian**

Have faith too in your personal judgement. We live in an age where everything is over-researched. *See, Feel, Think, Do* (subtitled *The Power Of Instinct In Business*) by Andy Milligan and Shaun Smith points out that research is only a rear-view mirror – it cannot tell you the potential effect of your business idea with any degree of accuracy. The only way you are going to find out is to get on and do it – a theme that we will come on to later. So if you think you have a brilliant idea, then scribble it down. By all means test-drive it on a respected friend, but don't dilute it, and don't doubt its value until you have investigated it yourself and found holes in it.

Why almost is more than enough

A lot of business advice tells you that only the best will do. I don't necessarily agree. I have met far too many people who still haven't quite launched their business because they are waiting for some apparently vital last piece of information. Three years later, they are still fiddling about. That's when the frustration kicks in. No, the successful businessperson forges something that is almost there and then gets on with it. That means getting it to market in one form or another as soon as is sensible and practical. Early customers will soon offer refinements to the basic idea, just as they do with open software on the Internet in the world of computers. If the basic idea is sound, people are only too happy to contribute ideas for improvement. By then, you are already underway, and may even have generated sufficient cash flow to fund any new developments without borrowing the money.

> *"People are always blaming their circumstances for what they are. I don't believe in circumstances. The people who get on in this world are the people who get up and look for the circumstances they want, and, if they can't find them, they make them."*
>
> **George Bernard Shaw**

So don't get too detailed and don't let circumstances prevent you from getting on with it. It's your job to create new circumstances by making a start.

Progress not perfection

Perfection never quite arrives. Too many businesses sit around pontificating about the so-called "perfect" solution that is just around the corner. The trouble is, around the corner is where it usually stays. Many Japanese companies practice *Kaizen*, the art of continual improvement involving everyone (managers and workers alike), but none of them ever claim they have it perfect. A summary of this and other business concepts can be found in *The Economist Guide To Management Ideas*, and in Appendix I.

So aim for progress, not perfection. It will get you far further than the pursuit of some business El Dorado that never arrives. A client of mine, Bruce Duckworth, has used this philosophy to good effect in his business. It stops his company being paralysed by the possibility of "just another thing" that will prevent progress. Another of his mantras is MAYA: "Most advanced yet acceptable". This approach encourages a business to push as far as it can, but stops short of neutering itself by refusing to proceed unless something is perfect. It may sound like a cop out, but it absolutely isn't. If you genuinely think you can find perfection, then hats off to you. More likely though, you will use the chimera of it as an excuse not to proceed, and that's no help to you at this critical early stage when the important thing is forward motion.

Beware spreadsheets

You must also keep a close eye on those nasty spreadsheets. No one ever said: *"Wow! What a great business! I wonder how many spreadsheets they got through to achieve that?"* Spreadsheets have their place in proving that your maths is accurate and that you are not going to go bust within weeks, but other than that, they can be a massive distraction. For the more anal amongst us, they seem to provide a sort of comfortable refuge where a person can hide amidst scores of different forecasts and projections. You know the sort of thing:

"Deep joy! I've got a bull forecast, a bear forecast, a grizzly bear forecast, an Armageddon scenario, three seasonally-adjusted scenarios, a stretch plan, a master stretch plan, and of course, a Big Willy world domination plan. That should keep the bank manager happy!"

Er, no, not really. The majority of forecasts are a collection of significantly inaccurate figures that never actually happen. The approximate shape that they generate can help very large and complex businesses, but are of less relevance to small ones because we are after simplicity and clarity so that you, the owner, can understand your own business easily. You are much better off with a simple plan and some clear numbers on one page. And that's what we are going to do now. Go on. Dare to be different.

> *"If everybody's thinking the same thing, then nobody's thinking."*
>
> **George Patton, quoted in the Pittsburgh Post-Gazette**

The one-page business plan

The one-page business plan is something I have used hundreds of times in training and teaching over the years. In many instances, people have been labouring for some time over the massive forms that the bank gave them to fill in. It's all too baffling and unnecessary. This simple plan unclogs it all. I even had an example recently where a friend had been slaving over her business plan for three months without really getting anywhere. This simple equation solved it in 20 minutes. So here we go. Start by having a quick look at Figure 2.1. You will need to be able to fill in these numbers to establish whether your business is likely to work or not.

Step 1: How much do I want to earn each year? _____

Step 2: A realistic expenditure per customer/visit/transaction/project is: _____

Step 3: A realistic number of customers/visits/transactions/projects is:

_____ per day
_____ per week
_____ per month
_____ per year

Step 4: How much money will this frequency generate?

£_____ per day
£_____ per week
£_____ per month
£_____ per year

Step 5: Now deduct all costs from the £ per year figure:

Per year total: £_____
Minus costs: £_____
Remaining: £_____

(If your salary is included in these costs, then make sure it equals the figure in Step 1. If it doesn't, see Step 6.)

Step 6: The figure remaining should equal or exceed the figure in Step 1. If it doesn't, change something. This could be:

- Expenditure per customer.
- Number of customers.
- Costs.
- The amount you want to earn each year (if you overshot a bit).
- All of the above.

Fig. 2.1:   The one-page business plan

Step 1: How much do I want to earn each year?

Okay, so let's walk through it now. Start by writing in the figure you want to earn. Amazingly, many people haven't even thought about this basic question, but you must. If you haven't a clue, skip ahead to the next section (*How much money do I really want?*) and then decide. Many of you will be thinking: how can I decide what I will earn when I haven't done the plan yet? Exactly, that's the whole point. Most business plans are unhelpful precisely *because* they build an income or profit figure from a set of hypothetical variables. That's useless to you if you want to work out whether your business will sustain you or deliver the income you want. There's no point in building a net that doesn't catch the right size of fish, so we're not going to design a business that isn't going to generate the money you want, because it won't even be worth starting.

> *"Good fortune is what happens when opportunity meets with planning."*
>
> **Thomas Eddison**

It's simple, but effective. That's why we are going to start at the end. So write down what you want to earn. This can either be the total profit at the end of the year that will go straight into your pocket as the sole owner of the business, or a decent salary paid for by the business. The net effect will be the same, and there is another question in the chain that flushes out whether you have got that bit wrong.

Step 2: A realistic expenditure per customer/visit/transaction/project

Now you need to take a stab at a realistic cost per customer, visit, transaction, project, or whatever the appropriate description is for the business that you intend to start. Let's take a couple of examples.

If you want to run a coffee shop, then you might put in £5 per visit. If you think your customers will only buy the one cup of coffee, then it might be just £1. If you think they will stay for breakfast, then £5 might be about right. If you are selling to a corporate market where visitors come in for hours on end and work on their computers, then it might be £10. You get the idea. That's your first example of price flexibility if you think creatively.

Or, if your business is installing boilers for central heating systems, then the price might be £2,000 per installation with a £250 mark-up for you. It's not my line so I don't know what the real figures are. It doesn't matter. You should know what it is for the line of business that you intend to establish, so you can fill them in reasonably accurately. The point is that no one would be selling boilers at the same frequency or price as cups of coffee, so work out the parameters that apply to your market and choose an appropriate average price per transaction.

Step 3: A realistic number of customers/visits/transactions/projects

This number will vary massively depending on the nature of your proposed business. The simplest way to do the calculation is to break it down into tiny units, and then build it back up again. Look at it by day, then multiply it by the number of days in a week, month or year that you will be trading. In the coffee shop example (see Figure 2.2), I have guesstimated that the business might sell 20 cups of coffee per hour in an 8-hour day. Assuming a 5-day week, allowing 4 weeks a month, and 1 month off for holiday, you can do the maths. Like this:

160 per day (assuming 20 per hour, and an 8-hour day)
800 per week (assuming 5 days a week)
3,200 per month
35,200 per year (assuming 1 month off for holiday)

Now you can begin to see how every variable is critical. If your pricing is wrong, then so is the whole model. If you open for an extra day per week, or hour per day, what happens to the figure? By the way, if you own a coffee shop and these figures are ludicrous, don't shoot the author – they are illustrative, not real.

Step 4: How much money will this frequency generate?

Once you have completed Step 3, it is a simple matter to multiply your figures by the price per customer, visit or transaction that you settled on in Step 2. In this example, it is:

£800 per day (assuming £5 per visit)
£4,000 per week
£16,000 per month
£176,000 per year (same assumptions as before)

This last "per year" figure is the big one you have been waiting for.

Step 5: Deduct all costs

Clearly, this total income figure is not profit, and does not immediately rocket into your pocket for your personal

Step 1: How much do I want to earn each year? £50,000

Step 2: A realistic expenditure per customer/visit/transaction is: £5

Step 3: A realistic number of customers/visits/transactions is:

160 per day (assuming 20 per hour, and an 8-hour day)
800 per week (assuming 5 days a week)
3200 per month
35,200 per year (assuming one month off for holiday)

Step 4: How much money will this frequency generate?

£800 per day (assuming £5 per visit)
£4,000 per week
£16,000 per month
£176,000 per year (same assumptions as before)

Step 5: Now deduct all costs from the £ per year figure:

Per year total: £176,000
Minus costs: £100,000
Remaining: £76,000

Step 6: The figure remaining exceeds the figure in Step 1 (£50,000),
so this plan works.

Fig. 2.2: Coffee shop example

pleasure. It is what the business takes in, not you personally.
Now you have to work out what your costs will be. There
are two basic ways of doing this:

1. Subtract from the expenditure per transaction every
   element of cost needed to fulfil that transaction. What's
   left is the margin. If there is nothing left, then your

pricing is wrong. For example, if you have a 20% margin on every coffee shop transaction, then for each one £4 is cost and £1 is margin.
2. Alternatively, look at the entire business over the whole year. Add up everything you will need to pay for. Now subtract that figure from the "per year" figure in Step 4.

The easier comparison is between the total year figure and the income ("per year") figure in Step 4. Clearly we want the income to be substantially larger than the costs in order to generate the profit you desire. In the coffee shop example in Figure 2.2, the costs are £100,000, so the surplus is £76,000 – well over the desired figure of £50,000 at the top. So that particular plan works.

Step 6: If it doesn't work, change something

So the figure remaining should equal or exceed the figure in Step 1. If it exceeds it, then you may well have a successful business model. If there is a ridiculously massive profit, then check your assumptions and figures again to be certain. If it doesn't equal or exceed your expectation, then don't panic yet, but you will have to change something. This could be:

- Expenditure per customer.
- Number of customers.
- Costs.
- The amount you want to earn each year (if you overshot a bit).
- Any combination, or all of the above.

This seems a simple list, but it includes a huge number of variables and assumptions, so take your time. You may find that you have incomplete information so you can't be sure of a certain figure. If so, go and find out otherwise you will be starting your business under false pretences, and the main person to suffer will be you.

Keep going and rework the plan frequently. If, after many attempts, it never generates the surplus that you want, then you may have to conclude that the proposed business isn't going to work.

Boiler installation example

The coffee shop owner had a model that worked, but frequently they don't, and it is best to know straight away before you waste too much time. Take a look at Figure 2.3, in which I have pursued the boiler installation example. The owner desires the same income, but the construction of the business is completely different. For ease of explanation, I am going to pretend that the owner is male. He is going to make £250 on every boiler installed, but the frequency of purchase is only three per week. Working the same number of days as the coffee shop owner, he is only generating £33,000 per year. His costs are lower at £10,000, but he is still left with only £23,000 against an aspiration of £50,000, so this model doesn't work, assuming his income desires haven't changed. The owner of this business needs to look again at all the variables in Step 6: the expenditure per customer, the number of possible customers, the costs and the amount he wants to earn each year. Tweaking any combination of these could still lead to a viable business.

So let's have a look at how a small change in the variables can make a huge difference. Increasing the number of transactions from three to five per week (i.e. one a day) automatically increases the income from £33,000 to £55,000.

Step 1: How much do I want to earn each year? £50,000

Step 2: A realistic expenditure per customer/visit/transaction
   is:£250*

*This is mark-up of £250 on a £2,000 boiler.

Step 3: A realistic number of customers/visits/transactions is:

3 per week (assuming 5 days a week)
12 per month
132 per year (assuming one month off for holiday)

Step 4: How much money will this frequency generate?

£750 per week
£3,000 per month
£33,000 per year (same assumptions as before)

Step 5: Now deduct all costs from the £ per year figure:

Per year total: £33,000
Minus costs: £10,000
Remaining: £23,000

Step 6: The figure is less than the figure in Step 1 (£50,000), so
the plan does not work. Something needs to change. This could be:

- Expenditure per customer.
- Number of customers.
- Costs.
- The amount you want to earn each year.
- All of the above.

Fig. 2.3:   Boiler installation example

If costs can then be halved from £10,000 to £5,000, then the target earning figure of £50,000 can indeed be achieved. Obviously this is hypothetical, but it demonstrates the inter-relationship between the variables. The maths would then look like in Figure 2.4.

How much money do I really want?

It sounds like a bit of a strange question, but it has to be addressed early otherwise you will just end up with a random amount which may or may not suit your needs. A lot of people simply don't like talking about money, but if you elect not to, then I can guarantee you one thing:

> *Those who choose not to talk about the money early on will always end up with less than they wanted.*

Deeply profound, or just common sense? You decide. As someone once said, the problem with common sense is that it is not all that common. Anyway, whether it is shyness, old-fashioned English reserve or whatever, you've got to work out the money early doors. That means working out how you are going to get paid, and what you are going to be left with at the end of all your efforts. The idea of working all year only to make a loss sounds ridiculous, but companies do it all the time. You only have to read a few annual reports or watch the news to know that.

When answering this question, lots of people look up with a twinkle in their eye and say something like: *"Well, a million pounds, obviously!"* But once they have overcome the split-second dream of a lottery-winning amount, they quickly knuckle down to a sensible figure based on an appropriate balance between what they need to earn and what they would like to increase it to in order to improve

Step 1: How much do I want to earn each year? £50,000

Step 2: A realistic expenditure per customer/visit/transaction is: £250

Step 3: A realistic number of customers/visits/transactions is:

5 per week (assuming 5 days a week)
20 per month
220 per year (assuming one month off for holiday)

Step 4: How much money will this frequency generate?

£1250 per week
£5,000 per month
£55,000 per year

Step 5: Now deduct all costs from the £ per year figure:

Per year total: £55,000
Minus costs: £5,000
Remaining: £50,000

Step 6: The figure is the same as the figure in Step 1 (£50,000), so the plan does work.

Fig. 2.4:   Revised boiler installation example

their lives. So just take a little time and work out what you would like. Then we can set about getting it.

If you are still having problems with the maths, there is another set of questions in Figure 2.5 to flush out whether your idea is viable or not. But for now let's get on and discuss what your business proposition is.

- What are you charging the customer?
- On what basis is this calculated?
- How is the work done equated to the price paid?
- What are the staff costs?
- What are the time costs?
- What are the material costs?
- What is the cost of sale?
- What is the margin?
- Is that viable for you?
- What aspects of these findings can you discuss with your customer?

Fig. 2.5:   How do you get paid?

What's the proposition?

The proposition is what you are offering as a business. It is essential that you become adept at describing what you do. For a quick rundown on this, do glance at *Teach Yourself Running Your Own Business*, page 49. Propositions vary hugely, from basic descriptions (*"I am a florist"*) to complicated technical stuff (*"We have the most advanced software platform in the call centre market, outperforming the ZX22 by a staggering 43%"*). Sole traders and those starting businesses will always want to be at the simpler end of this spectrum, because:

> *If you can't explain to a stranger what you do in 30 seconds, then you haven't got a business.*

Deciding on your proposition does not have to be complicated. In the same way that there are only a limited number of strategies in the world, there are only a limited

- Price.
- Results/reliability/guarantee/case histories.
- Exclusivity/specific market/niche.
- Service.
- Quality.
- Uniqueness/innovation/originality.
- Experience/image/qualifications.

Which apply to your business?

Fig. 2.6:   Possible sources of a unique selling proposition

number of propositions. Have a look at Figure 2.6 to gain a flavour of what yours might be and work through some possibilities.

To help you articulate these ideas, here are some examples based on a hypothetical business that sells apples:

Price: Adam's Apples are the cheapest/best value in town.
Results: Adam's Apples win more awards than any other.
Reliability: Adam's Apples are perfect every time.
Guarantee: If you aren't happy with Adam's Apples we'll give you your money back.
Case histories: The Queen used Adam's Apples at her coronation.
Exclusivity/specific market/niche: Only royalty use Adam's Apples.
Service: We will deliver Adam's Apples anywhere in the country.
Quality: Adam's Apples are the best in the country.
Uniqueness/innovation: Only Adam's Apples come from prize-winning orchards.

Originality: Adam's Apples were the first ever to be sold in the UK.

Experience: Adam's Apples has 500 years of growing experience.

Image: Adam's Apples are so trendy that they are eaten by the famous film star Johnny Glitterball.

Qualifications: Our master grower is the most fêted in the world.

Have a think about which characteristics are most appropriate for your market. Write it down as a complete sentence, and then read it out loud. If it sounds daft, then change it. When you are happy with a version, try it out on your partner, or your mum. They may say it is incomprehensible. This will be your first small example of rejection – see Chapter 8, dealing with setbacks.

Describe it to your mum

You may have heard this before, but it is absolutely essential that you can express what you do in the simplest possible terms. Do not succumb to the nasty modern trend to over-complicate things. It just doesn't work. People won't know what you are talking about and they'll think your business is the same as any other in your field.

> *"You do not really understand something unless you can explain it to your grandmother."*
> **Albert Einstein**

Well alright, it doesn't have to be your mother or your grandmother. Any family member or friend will do. The point is that what you are saying must be intelligible to any normal person. Keep It Simple and Sensible.

Beware the context

Testing your idea out on your mum is one thing. Going public with people you have never met before is quite a different thing altogether. Before you do this, have a careful think about how you come across, and make sure that the claim you are making about your business is suitable in relation to who you are and the context in which you are making it. Figure 2.7 provides an example of how this can all unravel. Imagine you meet someone at a party and they claim to be the most reliable builder in the world. If they are well groomed and their company has constructed a series of office blocks in London, then the claim may appear to be appropriate. If, as the example suggests, the claim is made by someone who seems rather dodgy, and the context is so ludicrous as to render it genuinely incredible, then the proposition does not fit the claimer, and will be exposed by the context.

Clearly the example is stretched to make a point, but it is important that the claim you make in your proposition is credible in relation to you, your skills and the context in

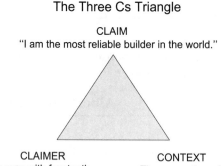

The Three Cs Triangle

CLAIM
"I am the most reliable builder in the world."

CLAIMER
A man with few teeth
covered in tattoos

CONTEXT
The renovation of
Tower Bridge

Fig. 2.7: The three Cs triangle

which the claim is likely to be made. Getting this balance right is important, and requires that you have a decent awareness of what you are like in other people's eyes, and how you come across.

Big or bold?

> *"The boldest measures are the safest."*
>
> **Chindit motto**

I saw this motto on a memorial statue in London a while back and thought it was great. A lot of business books will tell you to think big, and sometimes they might be right. But I have never felt that comfortable with "big" as an end in itself, particularly when it comes to running your own business. You will by definition start small, and a modest operation may be precisely what you need in order to have a thoroughly rewarding life with as little stress as possible (see the lifestyle versus build-to-sell debate in the next chapter).

Bold ideas are much more fun than big ones. If you can, do something radical and distinctive. This will make your proposition much more interesting, and be more likely to justify premium pricing. Of course, you will need to be braced for some strange reactions to your unusual idea.

> *"Every revolutionary idea evokes three stages of reaction:*
> *1) It's completely impossible;*
> *2) It's possible but it's not worth doing;*
> *3) I said it was a good idea all along."*
>
> **Arthur C. Clarke, quoted in The Times**

Don't worry though. Over time, if your idea is a good one, people will come round. Early detractors could even become your best advocates. People love to boast to others about clever new things they have apparently discovered all by themselves. These types of people could well be your future customers.

Small is good

Don't worry if your business idea and plan are small. If that suits you, then that's fine. There is far too much written about how businesses must chase scale to be successful. This kind of macho bragging doesn't really apply to small businesses. That's why they are called small businesses. So don't get carried away with a world domination plan, when what you actually need is something that's just big enough to sustain your ambitions and pay the bills. Here's an old joke:

Brash Texan: *"Boy, where I come from I can drive all day and still be on my own land."*

Disinterested Englishman: *"Yeah, I had a car like that once."*

This "small is beautiful" philosophy also applies to ideas for developing your business. You don't have to split the atom or reinvent the wheel. Just make small, helpful refinements and you will be emulating the *Kaizen* continual improvement principle we were looking at earlier in the chapter (*Progress not perfection*). For more on why the next big thing might be small, have a look at *Teach Yourself Growing Your Business*, page 33. Equally, don't worry if your business idea is fairly straightforward. That's fine, so long as the numbers add up. Remember, simple can often be brilliant.

So is it a goer then?

Around about now is when you need to take stock and decide whether you are going to start your business or not. You will have mapped out the rough shape of it, and hopefully not got hung up on everything being perfect. Then you will have verified that the numbers work. If not, you'll have reworked them several times until they do. (Clearly if they didn't work at all, then you may well have had to conclude that that particular business idea will not work.)

You should have a short, clear proposition that everyone can understand immediately. Remember the ducks? If they have been pecking away at your idea for months, then you'll end up with a lowest common denominator pale shadow of your shiny dream. That won't do. Keep it pure and unadulterated. By keeping faithful to the purity of the original idea, you will be able to tell people clearly what you are offering, and you will already have the confidence of knowing that the idea will indeed make money.

You would have thought that by now it's time to make the whole thing happen, but there is still one crucial thing left to do before you get properly underway. Before you actually launch the business, you need to predict how it is all going to end. Barmy? Pessimistic? Not in the slightest. It's absolutely vital. Now read Chapter 3.

> *"Taking stupid risks is what makes life worth living."*
>
> **Homer Simpson, quoted in The Sunday Times**

Chapter 2 checklist

1. Map out the rough shape of what you want your business to be.
2. Go for progress, not perfection.
3. Don't waste time waiting for the perfect model.
4. Avoid detailed spreadsheets unless they are critical to the nature of your business.
5. Complete the one-page business plan.
6. If it doesn't work, change something until it does, or choose a new idea.
7. Think carefully about how much money you really want.
8. Work hard on a clear, short proposition that you could describe to your mum.
9. Decide whether you are ready to go for it or not.
10. Be as bold as you can and don't dilute the idea.

> *"The beginning is half of every action."*
>
> **Greek proverb**

Lifestyle Or Build-to-sell?

This chapter covers predicting the end before you start. What type of business would you like? What do you wish to do with it eventually? If you want to sell, who will buy it? What exactly will they be buying? What price do you want?
How will you justify it? Will you be able to work for someone else during the earn-out period? What type of lifestyle do you want? How much time off do you want? Who else is involved? What happens if you get ill? Half-dead insurance and how it works. Complete the one-page personal plan. Now it's decision time.

Predicting the end before you start

Millions of people start businesses, and if you ask them why they did it, they will usually come up with the sort of answers we looked at in Chapter 1. That's great. The energy, the enthusiasm, the desire to do it better, the delirium of telling the big corporations where they can stick their pay cheque. I'm a huge fan. It's what gives the country character and makes the economy tick.

But if you ask someone where it is all going to end, they have a lot more trouble answering the question. Lots of people launch a business, but a few years later many of them don't know what to do with it. They have made the break and proved their point, and then they wonder what they should be doing next. This strange feeling does not happen straight away. It creeps up later on – perhaps after three, five or ten years, depending on how stimulating the new venture has been.

Now to be fair, many people launch their business saying that they want to sell it at some point in the future. The problem is that frequently they haven't worked out when, to whom, what the value will be, or how to structure the business appropriately in the meanwhile. Nor have they often compared this scenario with that of a lifestyle business that could have the potential to sustain them in a totally different way. So in this chapter we are going to bat these issues around so that you can be clear from the beginning about where you would like to end. This will help massively when you have to make important decisions about how you set the business up, and how you manage it along the way to your desired end point.

Here's an old Irish joke:

Tourist: *"Excuse me, can you tell me the way to Dublin?"*
Local Irishman: *"If I were you I wouldn't start from here."*

What type of business would you like?

There are essentially two types of self-owned business: lifestyle and build-to-sell. Let's look at the differences between them.

A lifestyle business sustains the lifestyle of the owner, and probably of their dependents. In many cases there are no other shareholders, so the owner can do exactly what they want. Sure, the worries are all theirs to shoulder, but then so are all the rewards. The owner can pay themselves any dividend they want anytime they want, so long as the business is generating sufficient money. (I am going to ignore examples where people have stolen phantom money that they haven't truly made through false borrowing or fraudulent accounting.)

You can work whatever hours you want, in any location. The entire thing can be designed around you. Want to work 10am till 3pm and do the school run? No problem. Want every Friday off to do an art course? Fine. Want two months off every year to travel? Okay. And so it goes on. You can work in the Outer Hebrides wearing just a string vest for all anyone cares, so long as you get the job done.

> *"Life is the sum of all your choices."*
>
> **Albert Camus**

It's fantastically liberating. If you decide to earn next to nothing one year because you want to sail round the world, then you can. You are totally in charge and can make all the decisions. If there's a hitch, however, it may become apparent at the end of it all. When you decide to stop working, or you can't work any more, then where does the money come from? We'll look at this a bit more later (*What happens if I get ill?*).

The second type of business is build-to-sell. In other words, you are building something that you intend to sell at some point. The plus point here is that once you have put all the effort in, you theoretically get a large sum of money at the end for all your efforts. However, the problems with this route are numerous. They include having no knowledge of who will buy it, what the price will be, what the conditions attached to the sale will be, and how to organize the business in the meanwhile. I have met many people who have been convinced that they are building a business, but are unable to answer these simple questions. We will look at all this too.

What do you wish to do with the business eventually?

We are going to use some questions to flush out which route you prefer, *before* you launch the business. The easiest way to get to the bottom of this is to imagine that you have chosen one approach or the other, and then see if you are happy with the answers to the questions.

> *"No one did anything great who did not do something ridiculous."*
>
> **Wittgenstein, quoted in The Independent**

There is no right or wrong, but if there is a cardinal sin, it is embarking on the whole business of starting your business without deciding which endgame you want. It may not sound like a big deal but, believe me, when you arrive at a certain moment a few years later, you will see that it is. Put simply, if you think it's a lifestyle business and rip all the money out of it, only to decide later that you want to sell, there will be nothing to sell. Equally, if you are building it to sell and trying to sustain a lifestyle at the same time, it won't work. So read on. We'll start with the build-to-sell end of things.

Five crucial build-to-sell questions

There are some crucial questions you really need to grapple with if you think that you will eventually want to sell your business. In the posh management books, they call these possibilities exit strategies. The trouble is, you often can't leave when you really want to, so the exit may well be further off than you think.

1. If you want to sell, who will buy?
2. What exactly will they be buying?
3. What price do you want?
4. How will you justify the price?
5. Will you be able to work for someone else during the earn-out period?

If you want to sell, who will buy?

It is absolutely extraordinary the number of people who intend to sell their business who cannot answer this question. They think that building a business with an income base will automatically appeal to some unknown potential buyer at some point in the future, but it may not. Thousands of businesses have a substantial income base and massive problems. These can include:

- The customers could disappear any minute.
- The business doesn't make a big enough profit.
- The business doesn't make a regular profit.
- The business isn't very well run.
- The business will be pointless without you personally.
- The market has moved on by the time you want to sell.

Any accountant or potential purchaser will spot these holes in a couple of minutes. Some business owners think that someone will buy because lots of other similar companies have been bought in their market recently. This could be a large self-deception. It may simply mean that the market is saturated and that the buying spree has finished.

Only 3% of UK businesses make it to 100 employees, so the chances of arriving at a saleable endgame are quite low. You need to review your market and work out who the possible purchasers are. Are there acquisitive holding companies operating in it? Are there venture capitalists hovering around your sector? Are there rivals who are expanding and might want to swallow you up to reduce their competition? Will they still be around and interested when you have built something worth buying? You need to think about all this carefully.

Take the time to write down all the possible acquirers of your business. If there are ten, then consider whether they will have the time, money or inclination to suit your needs. Then consider whether the timing you desire is likely to suit them. What if they go out of business or change their priorities before the proposed sale? Think hard. This will probably eliminate some of the candidates. If there are only a handful of names on the list, your chances are slim. If there is only one, it may well not happen. And if there are none, then you can't sell, can you?

What exactly will they be buying?

Some people swan around saying that they will be selling their business when there isn't actually anything to buy. This sounds insane. How can they be so misguided? The thing is that the business world is so full of machismo and hubris that it is entirely possible. You only have to look at Enron to know that. It goes on everywhere in the corporate world and sadly large chunks of it have now seeped into the small business sector. The fact of the matter is, someone will only buy your business if it will make them a lot of money, or if they genuinely believe that it will. Read this warning carefully.

WARNING:
PEOPLE ONLY BUY BUSINESSES TO MAKE A
STACK OF CASH

As far as the purchaser is concerned, the principle is incredibly simple. Show me your accounts and I will work out whether I can make a load of money out of it. Never forget this.

What price do you want?

Of those people rushing about saying that they will sell their business one day, many haven't even identified an amount. Those that have usually have an unrealistically inflated price in mind. I once advised someone who was running a loss-making business with an annual income of less than £50,000. When I asked what sale price they had in mind, the answer was £85 million. Honestly, you couldn't make this stuff up.

Another common flaw is failing to realize what sacrifices will need to be made in order to generate a suitable sale price. Take tax, for example. Those bragging that they have sold their business for £1 million do not receive the whole amount in the way that they so frequently imply in the pub. They immediately give 20–40% to the taxman. So that's £600,000–800,000. The payments will be staged, probably over three years. The last one will probably be based on performance, so if their company hasn't performed that well in the final stage, which often happens, then the price will come down. So the so-called millionaire may only have a fraction of that in their pocket – the same amount, quite possibly, as the person who hasn't sold their business.

> *"We're going to have to think anyway, so we may as well think big."*
>
> **Donald Trump**

How will you justify the price?

So how are you going to justify this massive sale price that you have in mind? Well, the potential purchaser will view it as a set of historical accounts, and then project what they can earn in the future. Take a look at Figure 3.1. Although there are occasional instances of businesses selling in the first few years, this is very unusual. Five years is a reasonable rule of thumb to regard as a minimum time period that the accountants will want to look at to prove that the business is worth buying – and this might be ten years, depending on the nature of your market. They will want to see a minimum of the last three years showing excellent profit. They will want assurances that this is a sustainable position that won't fall to bits when they buy. They will calculate a multiple of these profits to generate a possible price. This will most likely ensure that they get their money back within three years and start making a healthy profit thereafter. These are broad principles that make eminent sense. Why would they give you a truckload of cash if they weren't going to make some themselves?

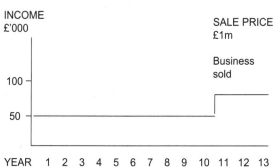

Fig. 3.1: Build-to-sell business

So Figure 3.1 shows your personal income deliberately kept low over a sustained period, such as ten years, in the interests of keeping costs down and in the hope of yielding a big payday at the end. There is a shock waiting though.

Will you be able to work for someone else during the earn-out period?

You've guessed it, when you have sold your business, they won't let you leave straight away. They're not stupid. Most businesses these days are people businesses. Why would they let the founder leave and risk major customers walking out too? No, they will tie you in for an earn-out period, typically three years, to protect their investment. So you have to ask yourself something absolutely fundamental:

CRUCIAL BUILD-TO-SELL QUESTION:
After working for myself for ten years, could I work for someone else?

I am not calling it one way or the other. All I will say is that I have observed a lot of horror stories where people selling their businesses do not get the money they want, and they get a lot of other hassle they didn't expect. Their desire to move on rapidly once they have sold can be very strong, particularly if they fall into the "I became unemployable" box that we examined in Chapter 1. Many cannot stand losing their autonomy overnight and just want to get away, even if they have to compromise on the final payout. Many walk out in dismay with much less than the sale price that they originally agreed. So think hard before you decide that you are building your business to sell.

Five crucial lifestyle questions

If you suspect that you might want to run a lifestyle business, here are some crucial questions you need to consider:

1. What type of lifestyle?
2. Is that realistic or too fanciful?
3. How much time off do I want?
4. Who else is involved?
5. What happens if I get ill?

Lifestyle is a bit of a hackneyed word, isn't it? I don't like it, but I really can't think of a better one that describes the phenomenon. Anyway, you know what I mean by it so it will have to do. A lifestyle business fits around whatever style of life you want. It doesn't pretend to be anything to anyone other than you, which is brilliant because you don't have to join in with all those corporate bragging games. You know the sort of thing:

"Seasonally adjusted, turnover is up by 3% year on year."
"Q3 is looking brilliant compared with Q2."
"We've just beaten the competition into oblivion."
"No one in our space can live with us."

To which the sole trader says: *So What?* (For a rundown on this and other questions that can help in business, have a look at my book of the same title.)

No, for most normal people a business is not a boasting platform. It's a means to sustain a living, hopefully in a manner that is reasonably pleasant. Sole traders don't give a monkey's what the other lot think, so long as they are alright themselves.

What type of lifestyle?

There's not much point in convincing yourself that you are Liberace and that you'll end up with a piano-shaped swimming pool when in truth you'll only have a few quid spare at the end of each month. Most of us are happy with a reasonably decent living and a bit of security for the people we love. If you are single, then that may well be yourself, and there's nothing wrong with that. The point is that you need enough to survive, a bit for your retirement and hopefully some surplus to have a nice time on the way. By all means design a plan that makes you a fortune, but don't assume it will happen as a matter of course.

Have a look at Figure 3.2 and map out a ten-year plan for yourself. Write in the amount you want to make each year, making sure that you allow for the tax you will have to pay and a reasonable surplus to plan for your old age and any holidays and hobbies. I have chosen an arbitrary straight line at £100,000, for reasons we will see later.

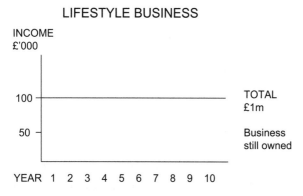

Fig. 3.2: Lifestyle business

If you can't decide on an annual figure, look back at the work you did for your one-page business plan in Chapter 2. If you are still not sure, try this basic set of questions. Remember, they are to do with you personally, and the needs of any dependents you may have, not the business income.

- What are my total annual costs?*
- What will my tax bill be?

- What do I want to set aside for my pension or savings?
- What is the likely cost of a suitable holiday?
- What extras would I like to add, such as health insurance or a new car?

*Take all your monthly bills, plus food, and multiply by twelve.

Add the costs to the tax and you have a must-have minimum income. That's not really a lifestyle business. That's more of a subsistence business. Now add the cost of contributing to your pension or savings, and a holiday, plus your wish list of new things. That's getting closer to a lifestyle figure for that particular year. But it's not until you are making a really decent surplus over a sustained period that you can really call it a fully-fledged lifestyle business. As a rough guide, that would be a 30% profit or more over three years. The only context in which this does not apply is if you actually don't want to make a surplus of money, in which case that's absolutely fine.

Is that realistic or too fanciful?

Some people fill in charts of this type and write in the most ludicrous figures. Some aim far too low and end up realizing that their business idea won't work and their household will be bankrupt in months. More commonly though, they put in ridiculously high figures that they have no hope of achieving. There is nothing wrong with setting your sights high, but you need to add a dash of realism too. Keep it sensible.

"Imagination is more important than knowledge."

Albert Einstein, quoted in The Times

How much time off do I want?

Another common mistake is to assume that you will be working every hour of the day, night, week, month or year. You won't. You may think that you will at the beginning. You may be fantastically hard-working. But one day you will fall over, exhausted or ill. That's no way to plan a business. No, you need to plan the rest periods in from the beginning. Work out when your customers do very little, and see if you can go away then. Is your business seasonal? There's no point in working when there's no one to do business with. Do you have hobbies? Then go away when the weather suits best. Do you have family? Then build in school half-terms or whatever suits the pattern. For a complete rundown on how to build time off into your year plan, have a look at *Teach Yourself Running Your Own Business,* page 113. This is absolutely essential for sole traders, because if you are shattered, then so is the business.

Who else is involved?

This leads to the fourth crucial question: who else is involved? By "involved", I don't necessarily mean in the business. I just mean anyone else whose quality of life could be affected by the manner in which you succeed or fail when running your business. If the answer is no one, then you can do what you like. You can go bankrupt, scrape by on a few bob a month, disappear for months on end – whatever you like. If so, by all means skip this bit. That's pretty rare though. Most of us have someone that matters.

Husbands, wives, partners and children are the obvious candidates, but there may be other dependents. Suddenly the question of whether this will be a lifestyle or build-to-sell business takes on a new perspective. If you run the business badly and end up with a tax bill that you can't pay, they could all suffer.

What happens if I get ill?

We touched on this just now. Many people who run their own businesses come a cropper when they fall ill. Of course, there are hundreds of different types of illness, but really they fall into three types:

1. Can't work for a bit.
2. Can't work in the same way I used to.
3. Can't work again, ever.

Not being able to work for a bit is usually tolerable. It might be a day off with a cold. Or a week off with a virus. Or even two weeks after you have broken a bone or two. But eventually you get back to work, and things are pretty much back to normal. However, if it's any longer than that, then the owner of their own business can really suffer, along with all their dependents. A month out of your own business could put a significant dent in the annual income, three months would take some recovering from, and anything over that could be fatal (to the business, not you). The next section tells you what to do about this possibility.

The second type of illness (not being able to work how you used to) is hugely significant for those whose stock in trade is manual work. If you are a decorator and you can't get up a ladder, then you may be up a particular creek without a certain implement. My nephew was a landscape gardener until he did his back in. He was in his twenties. You get the idea.

And then there is the extremely nasty third permutation where you can't work again, ever. That's where insurance kicks in.

Half-dead insurance

In the nicest possible sense, dying is no big deal in relation to being what I call half-dead. If you die, assuming you haven't left a trail of debts behind you, then you are not a liability. Your loved ones will mourn you and adjust. But if they were relying on you for income, and you can't work any more, but you are still alive, then you will rapidly drain any remaining money in the business and turn into a liability. Have you looked at hospital bills these days? That nest egg you have built up in the business will be gone within a year or two.

That's why I am a great advocate of "half-dead" insurance. Actually, the insurance companies don't call it that. They tend to call it Permanent Health Insurance or an Executive Income Replacement Plan. Who cares what it's called? The point is that, for a realistic monthly premium, it will pay you a sensible percentage of your monthly income for the rest of your life if you can't work. This is definitely worth considering if you are the sole breadwinner.

The one-page personal plan

So we have had a canter through the various issues that are likely to crop up depending on whether you decide to set up a lifestyle or a build-to-sell business. By the end of the chapter we will have drawn all those strands together, but now we need to take a quick look at the spiritual side of things. I want you to fill in the one-page personal plan in Figure 3.3. It works on the basic principle that there is no point in "fixing" the business when you are not content yourself.

I stand for . . .

I am at my best when . . .

In five years I would like to be . . .

My ultimate dream is . . .

I will never . . .

I am going to start doing . . .

I am going to stop doing . . .

I will continue doing . . .

Fig. 3.3:   The one-page personal plan

While you might feel a bit self-conscious doing such an exercise, I commend it to you as a good way of flushing out whether the business plan you are putting together represents a good fit with your private aspirations. If the two don't interlock well, then you may well have a problem. Anyway, the questions aren't that taxing. We just want to know what you stand for, when you are at your best, and what you would like to be doing in five years. The answers also allow you to work out what you don't want to do, and set some targets for the future. Strangely, things are more likely to happen when you write them down. The last three are there to help you concentrate on specifics that you need to stop, start or continue doing. So get a pen and paper, and fill them in.

Entrepreneurs: myth or reality?

I have never felt particularly comfortable with the term "entrepreneur". It is massively over-used and people often use it in the wrong context. For a start, so-called entrepreneurs rarely describe themselves as such. You can hear it now:

"Pleased to meet you, I'm an entrepreneur."

Er, no actually. It's a bit like me telling you that my trousers are cool. As soon as I say they are, they're not. So-called entrepreneurs may well do what the dictionary says: take some risks and use initiative, but then shouldn't everyone in business? If that's a definition, then anyone who has ever taken a risk is an entrepreneur, which can't be right.

Entrepreneur: 1. The owner or manager of a business enterprise who, by risk and initiative, attempts to make profits.
2. A middleman or commercial intermediary.
(From c.19 French entreprendre – to undertake)

Actually, I prefer the root of the original French word, to undertake. Apart from burying people, the more common meaning of the word is to get stuff done. Now that could well be the thing that distinguishes the person who runs their own business from one who doesn't. I bet they undertake things more often than some of their more sluggish corporate counterparts.

> *"Entrepreneurs are simply those who understand the difference between obstacle and opportunity and are able to turn both to their advantage."*
>
> **Victor Kiam**

Congratulations Mrs Duncan, it's an entrepreneur

Reams of stuff has been written about so-called entrepreneurs who were born that way, or destined to become so. A lot of this is nostalgia viewed through a Vaseline-covered lens. It's really not very complicated. Some people have great ideas but never do them, so they don't count. Others have lots of ideas and get a lot of them wrong. When they get one significantly right, they are called an entrepreneur. In truth though, all they did was get a lot done and keep going. They never gave up and they weren't bothered when someone else told them their idea was doomed to failure. A few float to the top and then we all rave about them as though they are miracle workers.

Fascinatingly, about a third of so-called "entrepreneurs" don't even want to grow their business beyond a certain size. Instead they prefer to pursue a better work/life balance so as not to "burn out". So entrepreneurs usually also have a healthy dose of humility. Have a look at Chapter 5 to see why this is an important component of a person who runs their own business.

Work out how

Just before you get carried away with your world domination plan, you might also want to know that between a third and a half of all people who run their own businesses found that growing it was much harder than starting up. Lack of cash, too much red tape and too little time are all cited as hindrances. Have a look in Appendix II at some of the hurdles people have had to overcome. So don't fall into the trap of having grandiose plans when you don't actually know how you are going to enact them. It is crucial that you know how you are going to get stuff done. If you need help, read the *How?* chapter in *So What?*

Decision time

Right. Now it's time to make your decision. Compare the two styles of running a business by looking back at Figures 3.1 and 3.2. In the build-to-sell version, you work your proverbials off for a sustained period, keep your costs as low as possible (including paying yourself), involve the accountants early, keep immaculate books, sell your business to someone you may or may not like, work under their new management for a while, and then disappear into the sunset a wealthy man or woman. Or so the story goes.

In the lifestyle version, you aim to generate enough activity and money to cover what you and your loved ones need, stick a bit away for the years to come, and do essentially what you want for years on end. Strangely enough, the amount of money earned over the equivalent time period could well end up being about the same.

Don't let me influence you. You choose.

Chapter 3 checklist

1. Predict the end before you start.
2. Decide what type of business you would like.
3. If it is build-to-sell, work out who will buy it.
4. What will they be buying and at what price?
5. Consider whether you would be able to work for someone else at the end.
6. If you want a lifestyle business, work out at what level.
7. Consider time off, illness and who else is involved.
8. Get some half-dead insurance.
9. Write out your one-page personal plan.
10. Work out how you are going to do it all.

Leap of Faith

This chapter says we have done enough talking, now let's get on with it. If you are still planning, you are still not earning. Phobology analyses what scares you most. The hardest things about starting: confidence crises, lack of support and what to do about it, sticking to your principles, and cash problems. Concentrate on action not activity. Test-driving the business is better than not driving at all. Don't do things the same way every time. Get the help you need. Screw it, just do it.

Enough talking, let's get on with it

Right, that's enough talking. It's now time to get on with it. The first three chapters should have forced you to think hard about your aspirations. Starting from scratch, making sure the whole thing wasn't pecked to death by ducks, then deciding whether this was going to be a lifestyle or build-to-sell business. But beyond a certain point there is no substitute for good old-fashioned action, and that's what this chapter is all about.

> *"To create real change, you have to become it."*
>
> **Ghandi**

We now need to get out of the planning phase and into the *"No, I really am doing it"* phase – not so much a phase as a new, and quite possibly permanent, way of life. We will deal with any fears and reservations you may have, to make it easier to make this crucial leap of faith. We will have a good old look at all the problems everyone in our survey had when they started, and try to learn from their mistakes, or at least try to make sure that these almost inevitable issues don't take you by surprise. We'll investigate how to stick to your principles when what you desperately need in the early days is just the money. And we will try to send you on your way with a spring in your stride.

If you are still planning, you are still not earning

Here's a bunch of irritating excuses for not getting things done:

"Project Cat Flap is still in the planning stage."
"The planning phase will be completed in Quarter Four."
"We'll go live when beta testing has ironed out any bugs in the system."
"We're still in a pre-test scenario."

You may well recognize this sort of phraseology from the corporate world. All it means is, watch my lips, *it isn't happening at the moment.* If it isn't happening, then it doesn't exist. If it doesn't exist, then no one can buy it. And if no one is buying it, then you haven't got any income. It's all pretty straightforward really. Put another way, the quickest way to get money is to generate some business.

> *"Success usually comes to those who are too busy to be looking for it."*
>
> **Henry David Thoreau**

This is of course blindingly obvious, and yet we all know people who are "still planning" their business. Some of them are actually too scared to start.

Phobology: what are you scared of?

These days, we are taught by the media to be afraid of pretty much everything. Global warming, obesity, anorexia, bird flu, mad cow disease, terrorism, tsunamis, nuts, you name it. It's a wonder anyone gets up in the morning at all. It's just too dangerous, isn't it? This is the industry of phobology, where everybody takes it upon themselves to scare everybody else witless. There are whole industries based on it – media, foods, fuels, advice and no end of pseudo-science. It's in all their interests to keep you scared so you pay more for what they are selling. A recent national research project conducted by McCann Erickson revealed that 72% of people believe that "Britain is more unstable now than it was at the start of the 21st century". One respondent even went so far as to say that "Fear is being sold to us".

> *"To the man who is afraid, everything rustles."*
>
> **Sophocles**

Cynical or realistic? You decide. But one thing is certain: there's no way you should let this fear culture affect your determination to make your business a success. Inform yourself of all the various pitfalls, by all means, but on no account should you allow misinformation and folklore wisdom to distract you from your chosen course. Being scared, paranoid or edgy should not be in the lexicon of anyone who aspires to run their own business. There will be bad times, yes, but good ones too. And if it's all plain sailing, you won't have any feeling of achievement, will you? So strap yourself in tight and get ready for a hugely absorbing rollercoaster ride.

> *"Paranoia means having all the facts."*
>
> **William Burroughs, quoted in the Melbourne Age**

The hardest things about starting

The second question in the survey was *What was the hardest thing about starting?* Here is a selection of answers (for the complete set, look in Appendix II):

- Cash flow.
- No pay cheque/giving up a big salary.
- Just doing it/making the leap.
- Working alone/personal isolation.
- Self-belief.
- Generating leads.
- First rejection.
- Uncertainty.
- Persuading early customers of my idea.
- People just buying "me".
- Having the confidence to hire.
- Finding good people.
- Lack of specialist expertise.
- No government departments can help because they have never done it.
- Delay between work and being paid.
- Balancing ethics of poaching old customers with need to eat.
- Being a lousy networker.
- Deciding on a name.
- Avoiding tax.
- Pricing.
- Not knowing where to start.

- Having a really slow start.
- Growing without compromising launch principles.

These observations fall into five main areas: confidence, support, principles, cash problems and actually getting on with it. Let's have a look at them one by one.

Confidence crises

So at some point quite early on, many people suffer from one or other of:

- Lack of self-belief.
- Uncertainty.
- Lack of specialist expertise.
- Persuading early customers of my idea.
- People just buying "me".
- First rejection.

Self-belief is an essential prerequisite of anyone starting a business, even if you have to face your demons in private. If you don't believe in yourself, then why should any potential customer? Take the time to work out what you are all about. You don't have to be improbably motivated like some missionary zealot on daytime American television, just a positive person who is keen to get things done. If you suffer from doubts, try to get them out of your system in your spare time. Part of the key to this may well be making sure that you take sufficient time off and spend time on your hobbies to provide a relaxing counterpoint to the stress of work.

> *"The more you learn the worse things get."*
>
> **Mark Twain, quoted in The Sunday Times**

Uncertainty is completely natural, and possibly even desirable. There is a school of thought that says that anyone confronted with a daunting task, such as playing a musical instrument live in front of 50,000 people or playing in a Cup Final at Wembley, performs better if they are slightly nervous. Those who are too laid-back can often be outperformed by those who are more on top of their game. So you probably should be slightly apprehensive. Uncertainty is endemic in business start-ups – you can't predict for sure how it will go. But what you can do is have a 100% bearing on your approach to it.

Lack of specialist expertise can be rectified by having a candid think about what you can't do, and finding out who can. Technical experts such as lawyers, accountants, IT specialists, bookkeepers, and so on can all be tracked down and engaged to do the things that you can't. There is also a massive element of "learn-as-you-go-along" when you run your own business – that's part of the fun.

Persuading early customers that your idea has merit is a tricky one. It rather depends how outlandish your idea is. If you are running a known service such as a garage or flower shop, then clearly it won't be a problem. But these days there are always developing technologies and strange areas that can be superb markets for new businesses. If this is the case, look carefully at the proposition work you did in Chapter 2, and make sure that your articulation of what you do is as clear as it can possibly be, particularly if your prospects include people who may not know the jargon well.

People just buying "me" is a common problem when people come out of a steady corporate environment. I have known all sorts of top professionals who have handled millions of pounds as directors or partners, and then as soon as they go out on their own they feel sheepish about charging sensible rates. It's as though the cocoon of the corporation was the only good thing about what they had to offer. This can't be right. The individual is equally as important as the company they represent, and that principle should be carried over with confidence into your new business, and the prices you charge. Have a look at the experiences of Rassami Hok Ljungberg and Peter Dann:

"The hardest thing was feeling and making others feel that I actually was good, and knew what I was doing. Also getting to grips with 'not working for someone else' but being proud of being independent, on my own. Not having a big corporate brand name to hide behind took some time getting used to as it had always been part of my identity. Now it was just me, and people had to buy 'just me'."

"The most difficult thing was the creeping awareness that it was now me alone that my clients were buying, and would they continue to? (This has still not left me!)"

And finally, how do you cope with your first rejection? Well, you dust yourself down and get on with the next thing. Have a look at Sheila Gimson's advice:

"Get back up fighting every time you're knocked down."

No corporation wins every contract it goes for, and neither will you as an individual. Keep an eye on how much time and emotional energy you invest in the pursuit of any one deal though. You need to have several things going on at any given time to avoid disappointment. Most sole traders will tell you that all the stuff they think will happen doesn't, and all sorts of other stuff that they never even thought of does. So rejection can be good because it liberates you to do the next thing. For more encouragement on this piece of reverse thinking, look at the best things in life in Chapter 6. The final point about rejection is that it is not personal – it's just business. So take the rejection on the chin and move on to the next thing.

Lack of support and what to do about it

Lots of people also suffer from lack of support in various ways, including:

- Working alone.
- Personal isolation.
- Being a lousy networker.
- Lack of government departmental help.

Working alone certainly isn't for everyone. If you really can't stand it, then don't design a business that demands it. Plenty of businesses have at their core personal interaction, whether that's every few minutes in a shop, every hour or so keeping appointments, or a meeting every now and then. Running your own business does not mean that you are sitting alone in a room all year. There's a massive difference between having plenty of solitary thinking time and choosing the frequency of your interaction with others, as opposed to being just plain lonely.

Personal isolation can, ironically, be achieved just as easily in a corporation – the "alone in a crowd" principle. One of the best things about working on your own is that you get to choose with whom you would like to interact, and with what frequency. The first thing you notice is that you can become much more socially reliable. There's no boss to make you stay late any more, so it's much easier to meet friends promptly in the evenings. If that's your bit of social interaction for the day, then what is wrong with that? It has to be better than being forced to spend time with people who aren't really your style.

> *"Anyone can sympathise with the sufferings of a friend; it requires a very fine nature to sympathise with a friend's success."*
>
> **Oscar Wilde, quoted in The Times**

Being a lousy networker was raised as a disadvantage by David Turner. Having a network performs two functions: one as a source of business and the other as a source of support. Most business books only concentrate on the source of business part, but I am more interested in the support network it provides. There is an unwritten code amongst sole traders that they will pass on any help they can. People really are remarkably generous with their time and advice. It's a kind of pay-it-forward principle that everyone seems to understand. Sole traders swap experiences, advice on how to deal with bad customers, let people borrow their stuff, perch in their offices, provide technical support, and much more. So it's your job to develop your network of contacts as much for your sanity as for potential business referral. Regard these people as your remote colleagues – always there to help, but hand-picked by you and far less annoying than many that you arbitrarily end up with in corporations.

One highly practical aspect of support, or the lack of it, is the lack of government departmental help. This was mentioned specifically by Tom Helliwell, who runs pubs:

"Unless you know someone that started running their own business there is no one to help you. The government

departments that are there to help have got no idea as not one of them has started their own business."

The problem with this type of supposed "support" is that the people providing whatever advice there is have probably never run a business themselves. Depending on the context, this lack of experience could well render their "support" totally useless to you. They might be able to tell you what the laws are, but at this early stage what you really need is someone who has been there and done it to help you along. So don't expect any particular trade body to offer this. Instead, seek out like-minded advisers who know what they are talking about.

Sticking to your principles

You have got to have founding principles when you start your business. It doesn't have to be highfaluting stuff like world peace or curing national poverty. I just mean the basic principles on which you will run your business: who you are prepared to do business with, minimum prices, the type of work you won't do, the speed with which you pay your suppliers, how you treat your customers, and so on. You need to decide this at the beginning because it will have a large bearing on how you come across and the likelihood of people using your services again – your repeat purchase potential.

There are, of course, two sides to principles: yours and theirs. The issues raised by our survey respondents quite neatly reflect these:

- Ethics of poaching old customers.
- Growing without compromising launch principles.

With regard to poaching old customers, the new business owner has an ethical dilemma. It is very common for someone to set up in business doing exactly what they did before, but as a sole trader rather than working for a corporation. If that is the case, then it is quite likely that the first few customers could well come from the contacts you already had from your previous job. You have to be careful here. There is nothing wrong with going for work that does not directly conflict with what your previous company offered. But there are plenty of people who have had non-compete clauses built into their severance deals, and you'd be a fool if you broke those. Your former company will almost certainly find out, and you can bet that it will have bigger and better legal resources than you. I have known many a fledgling business be floored by this in their first year, so if it is illegal, don't do it.

"An intellectually honest statesman changes his opinions but not his principles."

Sir Robert Peel, quoted in the Evening Standard

The other end of the spectrum is trying to retain your founding principles when the company grows. This is easier to keep tabs on if you never hire anybody, but even then it has its problems. Chances are that the type of customer you have when you start your business will be different from those you have in years four, five and six. Maybe, maybe not. But as the customers and contracts change, you may find your principles drifting. Every now and then you need to pause and check that you are still on your true course by looking back at the original idea that you dreamt up in Chapter 1.

Cash problems

Ah yes, the filthy lucre. People have terrible trouble with this, such as:

- Giving up a big salary.
- No pay cheque.
- Delay between work and being paid.
- Pricing.
- Avoiding tax.
- Cash flow.

Giving up a chunky salary can be a big deal, especially if you have become rather accustomed to the company car, the expense account, the pension contributions, and the hot and cold running secretaries. If you were pushed out of your cushy job, then fair enough. You'll just have to buckle down and make some adjustments. The rest of us have been coping without support for years! If it was you who elected to leave and set up your own business, then you should have thought of this little problem before you made the leap. Seriously though, if you have a good idea, work hard and apply yourself, and (crucially) do clever things with your tax, then you have every opportunity to have just as good a quality of life. If you don't genuinely believe it, then don't waste everybody's time – go and get another posh job with a salary. There is precious little in this book for you if you still want to work for the man.

Having no pay cheque is a slightly different matter. In this context, your pay cheque is synonymous with any income at all. The first thing to work out here is the time lag between the effort you put in and you getting paid. If you run a business where people pay you immediately, then you should be able to keep your income roughly in line with your outgoings. But if you provide advice of any kind, late payment can be a disaster. In *Teach Yourself Running Your Own Business* I tried to demonstrate the huge time lags between the work and the payment with the following hypothetical example:

Getting through to a prospective customer	2 weeks
Delay before you can meet	3 weeks
Rescheduling of meeting two or three times	3 weeks
Time for them to consider your proposal	6 weeks
Doing the job	3 weeks
Sending the bill out	1 week
Time taken for you to be paid	6 weeks
Total time	24 weeks (six months)

It really can take that long, so it pays to be aware of this in advance. Try to start with a small cushion at the beginning to soften the blow of delayed payment. If you can't, then have the money conversation early on to persuade your customers to pay you promptly. 50% upfront might be appropriate in certain circumstances.

Of course, you may develop money problems because you have got your pricing wrong. Careful work at the planning stage (the one-page business plan in Chapter 2) should have sorted this out. But if you find that you are simply not charging enough to cover your costs, then you need to change it straight away. The beauty of working for yourself is that you can reinvent yourself every morning (see Chapter 8).

Avoiding tax is another important issue. I am not proposing anything illegal here – simply that you become fully aware of all the rules and the opportunities to maximize your income. Remember not to regard the income as your money – it isn't. Make sure that you set up separate bank accounts for your personal and business use. Try to anticipate your tax bill and regularly put money into a separate account to allow for this. It's amazing the number of people who express surprise at the end of the year when they get their tax bill. Everyone knows they have to pay tax, and it only takes the simplest bit of maths to guess what the amount might be. To repeat:

WARNING:
THE INCOME IS NOT ALL YOURS.
AT LEAST 20% ALREADY BELONGS TO THE TAXMAN.

Cash flow problems afflict every start-up. As my old mate Paul Speers says, if you haven't had a bad debt then you haven't been in business. Don't expect any help from the banks though. They talk a good game when it comes to small businesses, but they don't really understand them, and they don't help much. Not one of our survey respondents has anything nice to say about them. The old-fashioned precept of your bank manager being an integral part of the community who would make informed decisions based on understanding of a local market and some knowledge of your integrity is long gone. These days, you are lucky if you can get to speak to anyone at all. So don't expect any help there. Just use your skill and judgement to organize your money sensibly so you don't get any nasty surprises.

> *"A bank is a place that will lend you money if you can prove you don't need it."*
>
> **Bob Hope**

Action not activity

And so to the overall theme of this chapter – taking the leap and getting on with it. People find this extraordinarily hard to do. Whereas in a company you can always blame someone else for inactivity, in your own business it all falls down to you. Look at some of the things our survey mentioned:

- Just doing it/making the leap.
- Deciding on a name.
- Not knowing where to start.
- Generating leads.
- Having a really slow start.
- Being a lousy networker.

> "Nothing is worth more than this day."
>
> **Johann von Goethe**

Whilst I appreciate that it may not necessarily help if a book keeps saying that you should just get on with it or make the leap, unfortunately there is no other way to phrase it. It is one of the hardest things to do when you are starting up. Have a look at the story of Chris Matthews:

"Just doing it. We have all met people who are going to start their own business 'one day', but who never ever get around to it. You can do all the planning and research you want (and you should invest time in this), but there comes a moment when you have to take a deep breath and get going. Sure, it involves risk. Yes, it involves cost. Yup, it could all go wrong. But if you don't stop dreaming and start doing, you will never know what you might achieve. As the ad says: 'Just do it'."

As he rightly says, we have all met people who are going to start their business 'one day', but who never quite get round to it. Don't let this be you. Idle people make useless sole traders. They deserve what they (don't) get. Have a look at Chapter 6 for more angles on why and how the right type of work really pays off.

Deciding on a name stumps some people. If this is holding you up, look back at Chapter 1. Not knowing where to start flummoxes others. My response to this is: start anywhere! It doesn't matter what order you do things in to start off with. Everything is equally important at the beginning.

Generating leads is another area that people find troublesome. An inability to get sufficient leads is often linked to being a poor networker, or being unwilling to put yourself about so that you meet plenty of people. We discussed this earlier in the chapter as a component of sociability, but now let's look at the business-generation aspect of it. First of all write down everyone you know who could put business your way. Then get in touch with them all. People often say to me that this is a daunting task. Well, yes and no. You can eat an elephant if you take it a mouthful at a time. Let's look at two simple questions to demonstrate how easy it all is:

Question	Answer
How long does it take to make fifty phone calls?	Less than a day.
How long does it take to have fifty meetings?	Less than a month.

It really isn't any more complicated than that. Put the work in, and the results will follow. If you are having a really slow start, then keep working at it until things happen. They always do.

Test-driving is better than not driving at all

Some people won't get in a car at all, or a plane. So they won't be going very far. But when it comes to your business, you have to get underway one way or another. There's no one else to blame if nothing happens. It's all down to you. So you might as well take a deep breath and get on with it. You don't have to be brilliant to start with, but you must start.

> *"Mistakes are the portals of discovery."*
>
> **James Joyce, quoted in The Times**

Making mistakes is all part of the ride. I am not suggesting that you immediately plough into the nearest wall, jeopardizing yourself and everybody else in the process. Just take it gently. Stay calm. Observe and learn from early experiences. Honing and refining your business is what will make it a pleasure, and, hopefully, a success.

Don't do things the same way every time

Part of the knack lies in variety. Don't do things the same way every time. You'll get bored for one thing. And for another, nothing will ever improve. Static businesses rapidly become dull and outdated. Whether that's a lack of new products, refinements of existing ones, new people, new markets, more outlets – it doesn't have to be relentless growth, but it should be a constant process of reinvention – have a look at Chapter 8.

Risking it all

Every year over half a million businesses launch without a word of advice from anyone. That's between 10 and 15% of all start-ups. Are they mad, or just full of conviction? That's a very hard one to call. With the benefit of hindsight you would certainly say that any business that subsequently failed (as many do) was nuts not to take advice. On the other hand, there's something highly infectious about anyone who has the courage of their convictions and just gets on with it. So I'll sit on the fence by saying that this is too hard to generalize about.

Get the help you need

However, I would definitely suggest that you get the help you know you need. What the level and extent of that help needs to be is up to you. You will certainly need the technical experts such as accountants and IT people. You can try to wing the rest, but do glance at some of the cautionary tales in Appendix II.

Screw it, let's do it

To conclude this chapter, let's take a little inspiration from a man who has been there and done it: Richard Branson. In his book *Screw It, Let's Do It*, he suggests that simple truths in life, and the right attitude, can inspire and enable you to do practically anything. People will always try to talk you out of ideas and say *"It can't be done"*, but if you have faith in yourself, it almost always can. I couldn't put it better.

This comes from a man who has made plenty of mistakes and taken a lot of risks. His main principles are just do it, have fun, be bold, challenge yourself and live the moment. He also proposes much softer elements such as value your family and friends, have respect for people and do some good for others. Have a look at the summary in Appendix I if you want to investigate more.

> *"An optimist was once described as someone who thinks the future is uncertain."*
>
> **Philip Bobbitt, quoted in The Spectator**

Just @*!`ing do it!

A friend of mine, Camilla Honey, runs a company called JFDI. It doesn't take much imagination to work out what it stands for. So what are you doing still reading this chapter? Go and get on with it!

> *"If you're going to do something, go start. Life's simpler than we sometimes can admit."*
>
> **Robert De Niro**

Chapter 4 checklist

1. Stop talking and planning: now get on with it.
2. Work out your fears and confront them.
3. Gain confidence from the experience of others.
4. Build yourself a support network.
5. Stick to your principles.
6. Concentrate on action not activity.

7. Test-drive things to get them underway (it's better than not driving at all).
8. Don't do things the same way every time.
9. Get the help you need.
10. Just @*!`ing do it!

Humility,
Honesty and
Humour

5

This chapter covers getting the character fit right, being humble more often, always being honest, and putting some humour into it. Only do business with people you like. Only do something if you know why you are doing it. Remember your personal plan. Understand the difference between service and servility. Getting your attitude right. How to conduct yourself. Wherever you go, try to lighten up the room. The four Hs: humility + honesty + humour = happiness.

Getting the character fit right

Humility, honesty and humour. What on earth have they got to do with making a success of starting a business? Well, quite a lot actually. There are hundreds of books on the market that tell you the structural aspects of setting up a company, but these can all be worth nothing if you aren't enjoying it or you can't cope. The three Hs – humility, honesty and humour – can have a huge bearing on how effective you are, and contribute significantly to a fourth one: happiness.

> *"Happiness is a way station between too much and too little."*
>
> **Channing Pollock, quoted in the Associated Press**

Being well adjusted helps you to cope with extremes, to laugh at mishaps and to shrug off adverse conditions. Humility, honesty and humour help massively in this struggle, and this chapter attempts to explain how. In essence, these qualities are your force field, and if you can get the hang of it, then lots of the other things in this book will seem easier to do, particularly when you are confronted by all the hard work and the inevitable early rejection.

Go humble more often

Humility, or the ability to be humble, may sound like a rather strange quality to recommend as a constituent part of business success, but let me explain. Humility has a number of subtly different meanings:

Humble: 1. Conscious of one's failings.
2. Unpretentious.
3. Deferential, servile.

Being conscious of one's failings is crucial. So is being unpretentious. Being servile, however, is not desirable, and we will have a look at what that means in a moment. Why is it helpful to be conscious of one's failings? The first reason is that it prevents you from convincing yourself that you are good at something when you may not be. This could be anything. Some people think they are good with other people when in fact others wouldn't agree. Some think they have great ideas when the evidence suggests otherwise. If you can admit to yourself that you shouldn't be doing the accounts, then you need to get an expert in. If you need a business partner, then find one that makes up for your weaknesses. If you hire people, don't hire ones that are exactly the same as you – they will just have the same weaknesses as you. The second reason is that it will prevent you from making inappropriate claims, like the builder in Chapter 2.

Lack of pretension is a highly desirable quality too. The business world these days is full of it – full of "better than thou" people, frequently with the condescending language to match. Starting your own business provides you with a genuinely unique opportunity to dispense with pretentious airs and graces. Many people leave the corporate world precisely to avoid pretension. If that is the case for you, then don't slip back into old ways. Don't design your new company in the style of the old one. Talk straight, and people will appreciate it hugely.

Honest: 1. Not given to lying, cheating, stealing.
2. Not false or misleading; genuine.
3. Just or fair.
4. Characterized by sincerity or candour.

Always be honest

As the old adage goes, if you never lie, then you don't have to remember what you have said. In his excellent book *Liar's Paradise*, Graham Edmonds reveals that 80% of companies think that they are fraud free, but a recent survey actually revealed fraud in 45% of them. His seven degrees of deceit range from white lies, fibs and bullshit to political and criminal lies. The ultimate lie is so large that it "must be true". As Joseph Goebbels said: *"If you tell a lie big enough and keep repeating it, people will eventually come to believe it."* It confirms what many of us suspect: that the workplace constantly bombards us with lies, fakery and spin. There is a summary in Appendix I.

> *"The truth is more important than the facts."*
>
> **Frank Lloyd Wright**

The basic principle of honesty applies to every aspect of your business. Here are a few examples:

- Pay your tax and VAT accurately and on time.
- Pay your suppliers on time and in full.
- Pass on discounts and cost savings to your customers.
- Do what you say you will.
- Deliver products and services on time.
- Turn up when you say you will.
- Call when you say you will.
- Never ever lie to anyone.

If you conduct yourself this way, you can't go badly wrong. I am not saying that you need to become a saint. Nor am I suggesting that you don't make a sensible amount of money. Just make sure that you treat others as you would hope to be treated yourself. There is not enough of this good behaviour around, and we need to start recapturing our integrity in business. There is no better time to start than now, and no more effective way than to enact these values through your very own business.

> *"Let unswerving integrity ever be your watchword."*
>
> **Bernard Baruch**

Whilst you may think that this advice takes the moral high ground, that isn't really the point. I am not on some messianic trip to clean up the world of business. The thing is that if you are honest you will have a more fulfilling time and a more successful business. A lot of stress is generated by people who are engaged in activities that are close to the edge. Questionable pricing, kickbacks, tax evasion, webs of deceit, siphoning off of funds – the list is long. Apart from the highest levels of organized crime, no one really starts out thinking that they will behave dishonestly. For many, it creeps up on them. Don't let it be you.

> *"Those that think it is permissible to tell white lies soon grow colour blind."*
>
> **Austin O'Malley**

Put some humour into it

Read any medical bulletin and it will tell you that a good laugh is good for your health. Besides which, it's much more fun. Who wants to do business with a curmudgeon? The world has its fair quota of dull, worthy business people, so why would you want to join in? There is no reason why business cannot be conducted in a highly professional manner, whilst at the same time being thoroughly enjoyable and, hopefully, a good laugh. Those who manage to achieve this balance have a better time of it, less stress, and are generally better company.

Humour: 1. The quality of being funny.
2. State of mind, temper, mood.

I am not suggesting that you need to wear a comedy nose all day or practice stand-up routines in front of the mirror to entertain your customers. Just view the world with a lighter touch. Awkward situations can be diffused brilliantly with a smile and a humorous attitude. As Steve Barber says, *"Treat everyone with the same respect and smile."*

> *"Common sense and a sense of humour are the same thing, moving at different speeds. A sense of humour is just common sense, dancing."*
>
> **William James, quoted in the St Paul Pioneer Press**

I love the idea that humour and common sense go hand in hand. Common sense is an absolutely vital ingredient in starting and running your business. And as we know, it isn't all that common. Suffice to say, a healthy sense of humour will allow you to view the world and all its madness with a wry smile. So when you have a problem with a customer, a dispute over money, a staff problem, a supplier issue or whatever, you will be able to see it for what it is: a temporary storm that can be resolved with a laugh and the right attitude.

Take the issues seriously, but not yourself.

Only do business with people you like

The word humour also refers to your state of mind, temper or mood. There are all sorts of ways in which this type of humour should be intrinsically built into how you set up and behave in your business. Your stance here will determine the nature of the people you do business with, the things you do, and the manner in which you do them. Your humour is linked to your self-respect and pride in your work.

> *"These are my principles and if you don't like them I have others."*
>
> **Groucho Marx, quoted in the Sunday Telegraph**

Groucho Marx was, of course, the champion of in-built contradictions. You may remember that he said he would never want to be a member of any club that would accept him. Similarly, by having a vast range of principles, you could technically try to please everybody all of the time. But you do need principles, as we established in

Chapter 3, and you need to be clear about what they are. If you don't stand for something, then you'll fall for anything, as the old bit of wisdom goes. It's not really for me to tell you specifically what these things are, but the overall point applies. Start by only doing business with people that you like. The smaller your business, the easier this is to apply. Life's too short to be dealing with rude people.

> *"Principles do not apply themselves."*
>
> **War memorial inscription, cited in the Mail On Sunday**

Only do something if you know why you are doing it

Keep on your course. Only do something if you know why you are doing it. If you know why you are doing something, then press on. If you don't know, then stop and reconsider. It's all about being more inquisitive and quizzical. There are few things more unfulfilling than doing something that appears to have no purpose. Although this sounds incredibly obvious, it is extraordinary how many people do things every day without really knowing why. Sometimes this may seem unavoidable if your boss has forced you to. But when you work for yourself, you become the sole judge of what is worth doing and what is not. This is quite a responsibility, but a great one if you think carefully and choose your tasks wisely. For a full treatise on the types of questions you need to ask yourself, have a look at my previous book *So What?*

Remember your personal plan

The personal plan you put together in Chapter 3 is a good anchor point for your integrity. The questions you posed and answered went to the very heart of what you and your business are all about. What do you stand for? When are you at your best? Where would you like to be in five years? What is your ultimate dream? What will you never do? What are you going to start, stop or continue doing? These are crucial questions and you need to know the answers.

Bear in mind that, although they will have provided you with an excellent starting point, the personal plan only serves its true purpose if you revisit it regularly. There are two important reasons for this. First, it is human nature to stray off course from time to time, so it provides a useful centre of gravity or moral compass for your life and business. Second, you may wish to revise your opinion every now and again. This does not mean that you are being inconsistent. In fact, it is probably desirable that your values evolve as you become more experienced and your business develops. So check back with the plan occasionally, and remind yourself what the critical qualities are that are central to your life and work.

The difference between service and servility

Part of the knack of keeping your dignity and self-respect is having the ability to distinguish between service and servility. Providing excellent service is clearly highly desirable. Being servile is not. It leads to terrible problems.

Service: An act of help or assistance.
Servile: Being obsequious or fawning in attitude or behaviour, or submissive.

Servility is pretty horrible really. You only have to look at some of the colourful phrases that have developed to describe it: toadying, sucking up, crawling, brown nosing, arse licking, boot licking, and so on. No one likes it, and it is not a successful business approach either. Servile people always charge too little. They generate little respect, and the customer comes back time and again to tread all over them. For full details of the horrors of BOHICA (*Bend Over Here It Comes Again*), go to Chapter 8.

> *"The minute you settle for less than you deserve, you get even less than you settled for."*
>
> **Maureen Dowd, quoted in**
> **The San Diego Union-Tribune**

Here is a list of unhelpful things that tend to happen to servile people:

- They tend to over-deliver.
- They tend to under-charge.
- They are not in control of their own direction or time.
- They frequently work evenings and weekends.
- They lack self-esteem.

What a hideous life! Don't under any circumstances intentionally arrange your business this way. Instead, concentrate on the positive aspects of providing excellent service. Your manifesto should read something like this:

- Your role is to provide top quality service without being servile.
- Your attitude is crucial to the provision of good service.
- If you are unhappy with your role, change something.
- If you are unhappy with a team issue, raise it and resolve it.
- If you are anxious about a customer issue, then tackle it head on.
- Good communication is vital to ensure misunderstandings are rare.
- Humour is a crucial pressure release valve.
- A dash of humility never goes astray.
- Always be honest.

As a simple exercise, try this approach to check whether you are striking an appropriate customer/service balance.

- Pretend that you are the customer and imagine what it would feel like to be on the receiving end of your approach.
- Is it good enough?
- Would you regard it favourably?
- Be honest in your assessment.
- If you don't like the findings, change your approach.

Getting your attitude right

> "Start off every day with a smile, and get it over with."
>
> **W.C. Fields, quoted in the Columbus Ohio Dispatch**

W.C. Fields was clearly a grumpy old man, but he makes an amusing point. Whether you are naturally charming or not, you need to get your attitude right in business. Regardless of whether your line of work is strictly in the service sector, you will be providing some kind of service, and you will not be successful if you carry a gloomy cloud around with you all day. Here are some broad guidelines to steer you towards an appropriate attitude:

- If your attitude isn't right, you will never get anything done successfully for yourself, let alone someone else.
- Be on the ball. If someone is spending money on your product or service, then they have bought the right to excellent service. It is your job to provide it.
- Be organized and efficient. If you are caught on the hop, explain your position politely, choose an appropriate delay time, and call them back when you say you will.
- If something changes after that, keep your customer informed of developments.
- Understand the value of politeness. Being polite gives you the licence to gain a little time and get out of sticky situations.
- Understand the crucial difference between service and being servile.
- Recognize the principle of service recovery. A customer well "recovered" after something has gone wrong can be up to fourteen times more loyal than one for whom nothing has gone wrong. Ironically, they can also turn into excellent ambassadors for what you do.

How to conduct yourself

> *"A man must swallow a toad in the morning if he is to be sure of not meeting with anything more disgusting in the day ahead."*
>
> **Nicolas de Chamfort, quoted in the**
> **Evening Standard**

A charming analogy, I am sure you'll agree, but the point does bear scrutiny. Human nature tends to put off the things that it thinks will be nasty. But often they turn out not to be. And in any case, when you run your own business, all the stuff has to be done for your own benefit anyway. My good friend Richard Hytner lives by the motto *"Do the worst first"*. It really works. If you do the tough stuff early, then the rest of the day is a breeze by comparison.

There is a whole chapter on appropriate conduct in *Teach Yourself Running Your Own Business*, but a quick review of the main themes is:

- You are the company culture.
- Subsume your ego.
- Do not distinguish between nice and nasty things to do.
- Remind yourself of all the positive things you have done.
- Never moan.
- Never finish a day before deciding what to do the next morning.
- Never do anything unless you know why you are doing it.
- Have reserve plans for every day.
- Remember that Plan B is often more productive than Plan A.
- Listen more than you talk.
- Be more positive than everyone else in every meeting.
- Never be late.
- Whatever you plan to do, start now.

Do a fraction of those things, and you will improve your attitude, your service delivery and your overall self-esteem.

Wherever you go, lighten up the room

Being more positive than everyone else is great fun. Try it. It's a darned sight more uplifting than being negative and contrasts brilliantly with all the moaners in the world, thereby making you much more distinctive than them. You may have heard the expression that someone "lit up" the room when they came in. That should become your objective wherever you go.

Wide berths and giving birth

In my advertising days I once walked into the office of a usually genial copywriter, who promptly bit my head off for no apparent reason. His colleague said: *"Ignore him, he's on the verge of an idea."* The moral of the story is: if someone is giving birth, then give them a wide berth. In other words, use your skill and judgement to avoid tricky conflicts when the timing is wrong. If someone is right in the middle of something, don't interrupt them. If they are massively busy, leave them alone. If you call someone, ask whether it is a convenient time to talk. If it isn't, call back later. Show a bit of sensitivity. People will appreciate it, and you will have less conflict.

Small house, big heart

A small geographical point, but if you work at home, spare a thought for everyone else around you. Many people starting businesses have other halves, and sometimes children, in and around them when they work. Try to work out calmly what and who goes where, and when, and get everybody to understand and agree what the rules are. With a bit of thought and a decent sense of humour, you can do amazing things in very small spaces. It can be done: I run my limited company from a couple of square feet in the bedroom. Everything and everyone can be fitted in, given a little give and take. As my housekeeper Ines says: *"Small house, big heart."*

The four Hs

> *"Set your sights high, otherwise the whole momentum collapses. Cherish your integrity and judgement. You can't work with one eye on the market, you have to stand for yourself."*
>
> **Theo Moorman**

The three Hs, leading to a fourth. Humility, honesty and humour lead to happiness. That's what this chapter has been all about. Set your standards high, keep them there and enact them every day. When you slip, check yourself, take a deep breath and get back up. There will be no boss looking over your shoulder to keep you on the straight and narrow, so you have to self-regulate. It may take a bit of work at the beginning, but the rewards are great.

THE ATTITUDE EQUATION
Humility + Honesty + Humour = Happiness

Chapter 5 checklist

1. Get the character fit right between you, your business and your customers.
2. Go humble more often than not.

3. Always be honest.
4. Put some humour into it.
5. Only do business with people you like.
6. Only do something if you know why you are doing it.
7. Remember what your personal plan says.
8. Know the difference between service and servility.
9. Wherever you go, try to lighten up the room.
10. Get your attitude right and conduct yourself well.

Hard Work
and Clever Work

This chapter covers the differences between work, hard work and clever work. When not to work hard, or at all. When laziness does work. Understanding the link between effort and results. Why lazy people achieve nothing. The best things in life. The good news awaiting you. Some simple early rules. Getting the money right.

What is hard work?

In this chapter we are going to have a look at the notion of hard work: what it means, and how to set about it. Don't worry, I won't be advocating a stringent work ethic, a nasty routine, or thumping the tub for a sweat shop approach. There's way too much macho opinion around that tells you to work all hours and become a millionaire. That's not really what running your own business is all about. You just want a realistic amount of reward, both financial and spiritual, for the effort you put in.

So the first question is: what is hard work? The word hard potentially has two meanings:

1. Mentally difficult.
2. Physically exhausting.

They are very different things. Mentally difficult work can be a pleasure. Repetitive factory jobs lead to boredom. No one likes doing the same thing all day. So variety is good, and often that will mean straying into areas where you are uncertain. Usually this is a good thing, because you get to do all sorts of new things, which keeps you alert and fresh. The only area where this doesn't work well is if you claim to be able to do something when you know very well that you can't. That's just plain lying, and we established in the last chapter that that's completely out of order. You can, however, listen to a customer's request and say: *"I can't do that, but I know a man who can."* That's what hundreds of modern loose networks do, referring work across different areas of expertise. Or you can say: *"I haven't done that before, but I think I know how to."* Many will be prepared to let you try.

Physically exhausting work is a completely different kettle of fish. The human body has limits. If your business is of a physical nature, such as construction, then you will need to work out these limits, and get in help when you reach them. Most tradespeople have got this down pat. Where it is harder to spot is with those who work long hours at non-manual labour. They think that they can do it because it's technically not physical work. And yet it is. Particularly when it is combined with an unhealthy dose of mental stress.

So when I say hard work, I don't mean silly hours, or anything beyond the sensible realms of what the human body can achieve. We are running a business here, not breaking some sort of world endurance record.

There's work and there's clever work

There is work and there is clever work. I never did like that Apple advertising campaign that told us to *Work Smart*. It really should have been *Work Smarter*, or even *Work More Smartly*, but there you go. So it's clever work we are after, not pure hard work. In his book *Simply Brilliant*, Fergus O'Connell points out that the best ideas aren't always complicated and the incredibly straightforward stuff is often overlooked in the search for a complex answer. Quite why people do this is beyond me. We looked in Chapter 2 at the pitfalls of over-complicated spreadsheets and so on. People seem to love them. But as Fergus points out, many smart people lack the set of essential skills that could roughly be described as "common sense".

You could do worse than follow his seven principles for attacking most everyday problems:

(1) Many things are simple – despite our tendency to complicate them.
(2) You need to know what you're trying to do – many don't.
(3) There is always a sequence of events – make the journey in your head.
(4) Things don't get done if people don't do them – strategic wafflers beware!
(5) Things rarely turn out as expected – so plan for the unexpected.
(6) Things either are or they aren't – don't fudge things.
(7) Look at things from other's point of view – it will help your expectations.

Another really helpful book is *Getting Things Done* by David Allen. He says that it is perfectly possible for a person to have a seemingly overwhelming number of things to do and still function productively with a clear head and a positive sense of relaxed control. His tips include:

- Only have one filing system.
- Turn your in-tray upside down and work on the principle of First In First Out (FIFO), not LIFO as many people do.
- Collect, process, organize, review, do.
- Nothing should take more than two minutes, nor go back into your in-tray.
- The four crucial factors are context, time, energy and priority.

If you have problems being organized and getting things done, this book will sort you out. The more relaxed you are, the more effective you will be (as in karate). Applied to all parts of your life, and not necessarily the most urgent bits, this becomes what he calls Black Belt Management. If you remember nothing else, just concentrate on the very next physical action required to move the situation forward. Both books are summarized in Appendix I.

When not to work hard, or at all

I can't put this simply enough: *there is no point in working if your customers aren't there.* I wrote about handling deadlines in *So What?* The two essential messages were:

1. Concentrate on the liveline, not the deadline.
2. Do not leave it to the last minute like an essay crisis.

The liveline is 99% of anything you do, whereas the deadline is the tiny bit at the end, so concentrate on the big bit. Many people claim that they work better under pressure, but I don't agree. The work is almost always of a lower standard. What these people mean is that they wish they could self-impose the discipline to simulate pressurized conditions, without actually having them. Any reasonably bright person should be able to do precisely that.

Take the time to look at cycles of activity in your business. Depending on the nature of your business, these could be:

- Time of day.
- Day of week.
- Week of month.
- Month of year.

There are enough variables there to make your head spin, but stick to bite-sized chunks. For example, if no one comes into your shop until 11am, then open at 11am, unless you can think of a brand new demand to fulfil in the hours before. If no one ever calls on a Friday, then always take Fridays off. If January and December are always dead, then leave the country. It's common sense. All sole traders know this. They have a daily feel for whether their customers are doing anything. So when your customers aren't working, don't work.

When laziness does work

In her book *Hello Laziness*, Corinne Maier suggests all sorts of subversive and sometimes amusing ways to do as little as possible. This is all very well in a corporation, and, dare I say it, a French one. Did you know that 75% of all French teenagers aspire to becoming a civil servant? Now there's ambition for you! The prospect of a guaranteed pension and an inability to get fired regardless of how lazy you are is just too much to resist.

But laziness needs to be approached with extreme caution when you are running your own business. Previous readers will know that I espouse a maxim that I inherited from my father:

Efficiency is a sophisticated form of laziness.

Those who don't listen attentively enough or think hard enough believe this to be an endorsement of laziness. It isn't. It merely encapsulates the idea that a well-organized person will generate more leisure time.

> *"It is impossible to enjoy idling thoroughly unless one has plenty of work to do."*
>
> **Jerome K. Jerome, quoted in The Sunday Times**

Jerome K. Jerome was clearly a professional idler, but his observations make an interesting point. Pleasure from leisure can only be derived if it offers a relaxing contrast to hard work. Those who hang around doing nothing all the time do not gain as much enjoyment from it because they have nothing with which to contrast it, and they certainly don't achieve very much.

> *"I like idling when I ought not to be idling, not when it is the only thing I have to do."*
>
> **Jerome K. Jerome, quoted in The Sunday Times**

In his book *How To Be A Complete And Utter Failure*, Steve McDermott suggests that the reader does the opposite of everything he recommends and they will be a great success. (The full title is *How To Be A Complete And Utter Failure In Life, Work And Everything*, subtitled *39-and-a-half steps to lasting underachievement*.) The steps he proposes include:

- Don't decide what you want.
- Don't do things on purpose.
- Don't know what you value in life.
- Don't put your goals in writing.
- Don't plan your priorities.
- Don't have a mentor.
- Don't take action right now.
- Don't get feedback.

- Don't adjust.
- Don't practice continuous improvement.
- Don't expand your comfort zone.
- Don't ask *"How do you do that?"*
- Don't commit to lifelong learning.

So here lies the debate. There will always be those who say that it's just not worth the effort. If you work for a corporation, then I suppose you might get away with a fair run of laziness, essentially being paid good money for doing not very much. Ultimately though, the most likely outcomes of this approach are:

(a) Boredom.
(b) No increase in money.
(c) Dismissal.

If that's what you fancy, then fine. But I doubt you do. Where "laziness" can be helpful is if you resist the temptation to exhaust yourself for no effective reason. Hard work for the sake of hard work isn't helpful.

Understanding the link between effort and results

It's all about understanding the link between the effort you put in and the results you get out of it. Doing vast amounts of work for little return, emotional or financial, is pointless. This may of course mean that you are doing the wrong types of thing, in which case you need to review the *nature* of what you are doing, not the amount. This is a point that many hard-working people fail to note. They think that because they are busy, they must be effective, but this is patently a non sequitur. In fact, the opposite may well apply: effective people have more spare time.

Why lazy people achieve nothing

Ultimately though, the point here is all about the effectiveness of you as a sole trader running your own business. In this context, there is no place for pure laziness. Put simply, if you do very little, then very little will get done. And very little effort almost certainly equals very little money. So you'd best get on with it.

> *"Do, or do not. There is no 'try'."*
>
> **Yoda (The Empire Strikes Back)**

The best things in life

Right, that's enough of me haranguing you about effort. Let's get positive and look at the rewards that judicious work can bring. In my survey, I asked people to say what the best thing about starting their own business has been. The answers are a source of inspiration, and give you a taste of the great things to come. They included:

- It's my destiny and I am fulfilling it.
- I am the architect of my own environment.
- I thought I could do it, and now I really know I can.
- I succeeded, so I proved I was right.
- "I told you so" is just as pleasing to say as an adult as it was as a child.
- Sense of pride and achievement.
- I have self-determination, freedom and independence.
- I have the capacity to earn more if I work harder.
- The variety is brilliant.
- Keeps you fresh and on the edge.
- Learning new things.
- Making interesting connections.

- The unknown.
- What you think is going to happen isn't. What you don't does.
- Watching a team growing is great.
- The harder you work the luckier you get.

It's a wonderful, celebratory list, isn't it? You will have gathered by now that I am a massive fan of small businesses and the people who set them up. These types of comment provide some clues as to why. People in large corporations simply do not use this type of language. They talk of missions and visions and campaigns, but the small businessperson just talks straight and gets on with it. They don't use excuses.

> *"Ninety-nine per cent of failures come from people who have the habit of making excuses."*
>
> **George Washington Carver, quoted in the Fort Lauderdale Sun-Sentinel**

So the world that awaits you as a reward for your efforts has some wonderful facets. Having the feeling that you are fulfilling some sort of destiny is great. Plus, the sneaking feeling that you just want to say *"I told you so"* to people who doubted your abilities. Just take a look at what Vanessa Dalton has to say:

"Realising you can do it and telling people that you run your own business. And yes, proving to those around you that were sceptical about your decision to go it alone. I have discovered that 'I told you so' is just as pleasing to say as an adult as it was as a child. I haven't actually said it but thought it many times when witnessing the looks on those doubting Thomas's faces when I answer the 'How's it going?' question."

Her full story is in Appendix II. Proving that you can do it can of course remain an unsaid emotion, and in most cases I am sure that is the right thing to do. But do enjoy the sensation in private – you can't beat it. And there's a lot more. Having the capacity to earn more if you work harder, the variety that keeps you fresh, learning new things and making interesting connections are all excellent incentives.

Then there is the great unknown. Scary or brilliant? You decide! We looked at different perspectives on this in Chapter 4. Suffice to say that what you think is going to happen probably isn't, and what you don't usually does. Get used to the uncertainty, cherish the variety, and enjoy the rollercoaster ride.

> *"The harder you work the luckier you get."*
>
> **Daf Jones***

*Daf isn't famous. His story is in Appendix II. His comment echoes one of the most quoted aphorisms of post-war sport, originally by Gary Player, "The harder you practice, the luckier you get."

Some simple early rules

Here are some simple early rules that might help to direct your efforts:

- Commit to quality early.
- Home in on the things that really matter.
- Avoid getting bogged down with too much structure and process.

- Educate customers to pay properly for your services.
- Get the money right.
- Only recruit people who can teach you what you don't know.
- Grow slowly.
- Keep your ego out of it.

There's no rocket science here, but do consider the negative displacement effect of doing the opposite of what these rules propose:

- Producing substandard stuff.
- Getting distracted by trivia.
- Under-charging.
- Recruiting people who are exactly the same as you.
- Over-stretching yourself too early.
- Being big-headed.

The point is clearly made, and doesn't need much further comment. A quick word though on some aspects of getting the money right, because it is directly related to the work you put in.

Getting the money right

It's all about balance. We all need some money to survive, and hopefully a bit spare to do some enjoyable things too. You can't get away from it, but you can get your head straight when it comes to dealing with it.

> *"Run for your life from any man who tells you that money is evil."*
>
> **Ayn Rand, quoted in The Observer**

Here are some important pointers to help you get the money right:

- Concentrate on the money, but don't become obsessed with it.
- Weigh up the service vs. product distinction.

The first point is self-explanatory. Keep an eye on it, but don't become a money bore. The second point is all to do with the difference between what you can charge for products and services. Products are materials that can be subjected to a mark-up. Services can be charged at a near-infinite margin, depending on the problem they are solving. Think carefully about the difference between the two in your market.

> *"You never realise how short a month is until you pay alimony."*
>
> **Old joke, quoted in the Mail On Sunday**

- Get your circumstances right.
- Try to avoid the most time-consuming issue ever: other people.

Think carefully about the financial aspects of where you work. Try to spend as little money as possible to start with so you can find your feet and get some early income whilst keeping your outgoings under control. Do as much yourself as you can. People issues can be massively time-consuming, and time is money.

> *"When a fellow says it ain't the money but the principle, it's the money."*
>
> **Frank McKinney Hubbard, quoted in The Times**

- The price/quality equation: if you cost a lot, you must be good.
- Aim for 50% repeat business within three years.

Don't charge too little for what you do. This is one of the most common mistakes that people make at the beginning. Choose a fair, preferably premium, price and stick to it. Deliver good things, and work to create repeat business. Repeat business is cheaper to gain than brand new business.

> *"The two most beautiful words in the English language are cheque enclosed."*
>
> **Dorothy Parker, quoted in The Times**

- Don't be small-minded about money.
- Be canny about requests for free "win only" work.

Don't waste money, but equally don't be tight-fisted. If you need to invest a bit to accumulate, then do. Treat others as you would hope to be treated. Buy them lunch. Be as generous as you would be socially. The rewards will come. But keep an eye on naughty requests for free work, particularly "win only" deals, where you only get paid if your customer wins a client of their own. This is no way to launch your business. There will be plenty of time later for charity and pro bono work, so don't bankrupt yourself before you ever reach that stage.

> *"I'm living so far beyond my income that we may almost be said to be living apart."*
>
> **e.e.cummings, quoted in the San Francisco Chronicle**

So there you have it. There's work and there's clever work. Don't bust your boiler doing futile things when judicious effort in a carefully considered place will yield the same, or even more effective, results. Don't confuse long hours with effectiveness – they are not the same thing. And although it may be a little late now, do bear in mind that if you are essentially lazy then you are unlikely to be a success running your own business.

Chapter 6 checklist

1. Put in plenty of effort, but do it judiciously.
2. Distinguish between long hours and clever use of time.
3. Include relaxation and time off in your plan.
4. Don't work flat out when · your customers aren't around.
5. Don't be lazy or you will achieve nothing.
6. Work out the link between effort and results.
7. Draw inspiration from the great things ahead.
8. Try to set up some simple early rules.
9. Keep an eye on the money.
10. Don't compromise your standards in the early days.

Gaining Speed and Losing Altitude

7

This chapter covers the dangers of gaining speed whilst losing altitude. Speed: good or bad? Busier doesn't always mean better. If it's not working, admit it. Work out when to quit, change direction and move on. Predicting pitfalls before they happen. Tripwires and predictions. How to identify your hates, then ditch them. Facing up to failure. Spotting fool's gold. Don't kid yourself, and don't mislead others.

Gaining speed and losing altitude

In their book *Juicing the Orange*, Pat Fallon and Fred Senn describe a gifted employee who was a nightmare to work with. When the president of Porsche suggested some amendments to his copy, he started a phone fight. The client terminated the call by saying: *"This conversation is gaining speed and losing altitude."* This chapter is all about not letting things get out of hand. There is a lot of emotion invested in a start-up business, and it takes a significant amount of humour and self-control to keep things calm. We looked in Chapter 5 at humour *per se*, but now I want to examine how frantic behaviour can ruin your business. Or, put more constructively, how careful thought about all your activities could make your life so much easier.

Speed: good or bad?

Some people just seem to be in a frantic rush all the time. Depending on the culture of a company, this is often seen as highly beneficial. You only have to look at much of the language of business to see that it is often admired:

"He's a man on a mission."
"She's really driven."

"That guy knows where he is heading."
"There's a woman in a hurry."

The question is: how important is the speed part? Speed may or may not be good. If it is a case of doing simple things rapidly and with the minimum of fuss, then speed is good. If it means rushing into big decisions without much thought, or for inappropriate reasons, then speed is bad. Mind your speed, and the nature of it.

Busier doesn't always mean better

Gaining speed in a business can often mean becoming more and more frantic. If your company growth is rapid and you now have lots of staff, then increased speed, in the sense of rapid delivery to your market, may possibly be a good thing. More likely, however, rushing at high speed will lead to a crash of some kind. Being busier does not always mean being better. As the owner of the business, it is your job to judge an appropriate workload for your business, in as suitable a time frame as possible. Think carefully about how fast the business can run. Don't over-stretch. Don't be greedy. Have ambitions for it, by all means, but don't sink the boat before it can complete its voyage.

Digging a deeper hole

The man in the Porsche conversation was being stubborn, probably rude, and was definitely unhelpful to an important customer. That is poor behaviour. If something isn't going well in your business, then consider mature ways of improving it. It may feel like a climb-down or a compromise, but it may well be better in the long run. You don't have to win every battle in order to win the war in the longer term.

> *"Compromise is the sense of being bitten in half by a shark, instead of being swallowed whole."*
>
> **P.J. O'Rourke**

At one point or another, you will encounter a significant problem. There will be an impasse on something such as terms of business, timing, budget levels, cost control, resource, the quality of materials, administration, or something as simple as attitude. This is when you have to work out how deep a hole you would like to dig. If you agree with the broad principle that the customer is always right, then it will be your job to sort it out. That will probably mean some form of compromise. So if something has gone wrong, then take the grown-up view and deal with it. An apology usually does the trick. Don't go point scoring or trying to prove you were right. Just look at the issue as though you were a neutral, and give the customer the benefit of the doubt. Occasionally, you will have to show a little bit of give-and-take on your principles. That's fine, so long as the main theme and direction of your business remains intact, which it will if you nip these smaller issues in the bud early on. If the hole is getting bigger, then stop digging – you can't carry on forever otherwise you will never get out.

If it's not working, admit it

Rather more fundamentally, there may be times when the reason things are proving to be unsatisfactory is actually down to what your business does, and how well it does it. It isn't easy to admit that one of your products or services isn't actually very good, or isn't working particularly well. If this is the case, then customers will be voting with their feet or complaining regularly. In these circumstances it really pays you to admit that something is not working, and set about fixing it. In extreme cases, this may mean withdrawing the product or service altogether. It may mean altering a fundamental element such as price or content. Or it may mean a small adjustment. The point is: you can't just stumble blindly along as though nothing is wrong, since it clearly is. You need the grace and maturity to recognize the problem for what it is, and sort it out appropriately.

Working out when to quit

This far down the line, it is to be hoped that your business is working well. That means that most of the things you offer should have been tried and tested, so that there are not too many surprises. But things change, and you may find that previously successful ideas fall out of favour. Competition can be a big problem here. If you run a coffee shop and Starbucks opens up next door to you, then you may not be able to cope. If you run a music store and now everybody is buying online, then ditto. It may not have been something that you could necessarily have foreseen.

> "When written in Chinese, the word 'crisis' is composed of two characters. One represents danger, and the other represents opportunity."
>
> **John F. Kennedy**

Problems, however, do lead to opportunities. We have to be careful with the language here though. I am not a fan of the relentlessly positive mantra: *"There are no problems – only opportunities."* This comes across as far too glib for my liking. Of course there are problems, and sometimes they are massive. And the smaller your business, the bigger they appear. I suspect that this rather pat phrase is used predominantly by people whose livelihood does not fundamentally depend upon the successful resolution of the problem in question. There's nothing wrong with admitting that something is a big problem, in fact it is highly desirable to acknowledge it for what it is rather than sweeping it under the carpet. There is no merit in ignoring the elephant standing in the room. If you can see it for what it is, then you can tackle it.

The crucial point is to get on and do something about it. Wallowing in self-pity is useless to the sole trader, as well as being hugely irritating to everyone else who comes into contact with them. If you have ever had a friend or family member who loves to moan, you'll know what I mean. Nobody wants to be on the receiving end of this, so make it your job to confront the issue and dream up a sensible solution.

Change direction and move on

The solution will most likely involve some change of direction. If the problem is fundamental to your business, then a total change of direction may be needed, and that is a very hard thing to do. At its most extreme, this may mean having to admit that your business is doomed, and having to work out a new means of making a living. Although potentially demoralizing, this may well not be as disastrous as you first thought. Problems can indeed lead to opportunity.

Predicting pitfalls before they happen

Far preferable though is to work out what is going to go wrong, *before* it does. This may not be as hard as it sounds. It is very unusual in business for someone to have absolutely no idea that something is going to go wrong. I am not talking here about natural disasters such as hurricanes and floods, although many businesses even insure against those. I am referring to sales falls, invoices not being paid, staff resigning, suppliers failing to deliver, and so on.

> *"When you are skinning your customers, you should leave some skin on to grow so that you can skin them again."*
>
> **Nikita Khrushchev**

This sort of stuff is much easier to predict than many people will have you believe. If your customer base is dwindling, then you will begin to see it. If you have pushed your pricing too high, you will see the effect in sales and hear customer comments. If there is staff discontentment, then you should have your ears open enough to be aware of it. In all honesty, the only problems you may not feel you can predict are the ones that you simply refuse to admit to, or when you will not listen.

Tripwires and predictions

Take a piece of paper and answer these questions:

- What worries you most about the business?
- What is most likely to go wrong soon?
- What early warning signs can you see?

This exercise is not designed to scare you witless. Try to do it when the business is actually going rather well. That way you will be in a more objective frame of mind. Equally, don't be a pessimist about it. We don't want a doom-laden list of things that, in all probability, will never happen, such as being struck by lightning.

> *"Fortune knocks but once, but misfortune has more patience."*
>
> **Laurence J. Peter, quoted in**
> **United Press International**

Review the list. Assuming it contains some perfectly reasonable possibilities, you should be able to think through possible approaches to fending them off. In the same way that

Prediction	Possible tripwires
Major customer moving on	1) Relationship review six months before
	2) Look for another before it does
	3) Change nature of contract
Collapse of market	1) Look for different markets
	2) Look for similar customers elsewhere
	3) Speed up/bring forward sales process
Bad debt	1) Insist on payment upfront
	2) Place money in an escrow account*
	3) Official credit check

*An escrow account is one in which money is placed to prove that it is there. The person or company providing the product or service can therefore see that the money exists and so not run the risk of not being paid.

Fig. 7.1:   Predictions and tripwires

doctors say that prevention is better than cure, we want to predict the possible problem, and put a potential remedy in place now. Take each of your predictions about what might go wrong, and now write an equivalent tripwire alongside it. See Figure 7.1. A tripwire is a reminder to nip a problem in the bud, or a measure to solve it before it happens (*see Teach Yourself Growing Your Business,* page 115).

Identify your hates, then ditch them

There are times when it becomes apparent that no amount of effort on your behalf will make the slightest bit of difference to a bad situation. If this truly is the state of affairs, then there may be a case for ditching them altogether. Who are *they?* Let's look at some examples. If you absolutely hate dealing with a particular supplier and the feeling will not go away, then ditch them. If you cannot stand a certain customer, then don't do business with them. If you don't like a market you operate in, then get out of it. If you don't like a product or service that you currently offer, then withdraw it.

A hate list isn't as vicious as it sounds. It doesn't have to be directed at people. It is equally effective at weeding out things that you can't stand doing. There is no point in deliberately engineering things you hate into your working life. After all, it's your business. So take a piece of paper and write at the top "*I hate...*" When you have had some thoughts, work back through them and decide which of them you can ditch. You'll feel so much better.

Facing up to failure

Fear of failure is natural, and we looked at some of the possible outcomes and consequences in Chapter 4. Failure is, however, an essential part of running your own business. None of us are successful at everything all the time. It simply isn't possible. So if your list of predictions includes a lot of possible failures, don't beat yourself up – it's just life.

> "Success is the point of self-deception. Failure is the point of self-knowledge."
>
> **Graham Greene, quoted in the Mail On Sunday**

Having said that, I am not suggesting that you only predict failures. If you are genuinely only able to write down bad things about your business, then it may well be a poor business. One would hope by now that you have been through enough hoops and careful thinking to ensure that this is not the case. More likely, there should be a healthy balance of excellent things that could go really well, and a few things that may go wrong. That's normal. As Graham Greene points out, those little failures are the points at which you learn so much more about yourself and your business. Increased self-knowledge will certainly contribute to a more fulfilling life. Equally, "success" is the point at which you may well deceive yourself.

Spotting fool's gold

Part of your growing maturity as the owner of a business should be the ability to spot fool's gold. Originally fool's gold was any yellow mineral such as pyrite or chalcopyrite that could be mistaken for true gold. Failure to spot the difference was hardly a cardinal sin, but an error that could be rectified with experience. Naïve people rush in. There's nothing wrong with being fast, but being first to exploit an inappropriate opportunity doesn't make the opportunity any more appropriate. A bad idea remains bad no matter when you arrive at it. Take the extra bit of thinking time to contemplate whether the "opportunity" or "idea" is actually fool's gold. Bear in mind in particular the distorting effect that greed can have. The belief that you can make a packet out of something may cloud your more objective mind. Beware of that.

Beware self-deception

Also beware self-deception when you are considering your business plans. It won't serve you well at all. There is a significant difference between self-deception and self-confidence. The former is unhelpful and the latter is essential. And yet the two are often confused. A self-confident person running their own business is able to keep their motivation high, and inspire their customers and staff. They are not fooling themselves at all. They have thought things through carefully, and can thus proceed with a high degree of confidence. That's completely different from people who have convinced themselves of the value of something without investigating it properly, and who then charge into the market with misplaced optimism.

Don't kid yourself

Not kidding yourself is therefore a vital ingredient of the person who runs their own business. Self-delusion just never gets you anywhere in the long run. It might keep you perky for a short while, but the ending is always the same – disappointment. Diving in to a misguided project may gain you some short-term speed, but ultimately it will reduce the altitude of your business. An ability to face facts is a critical component of this ability.

Facts I must face	How I am going to deal with it
Margin is too low	1) Put prices up
	2) Improve efficiency
	3) Move to more rewarding sectors
Business is too slow	1) Embark on a new business drive
	2) Run a promotion
	3) Work harder
Market can't sustain my business	1) Change market
	2) Start different business
	3) Move to different region

Fig. 7.2: Facing facts

YOU CAN'T DEAL WITH THE FACTS IF YOU CAN'T FACE THEM.

Facing the facts is well over half the problem solved. How to deal with those facts should come reasonably easily if you know your business well, which you should by now. Have a look at Figure 7.2. On the left-hand side of a sheet of paper write down the facts you must face. Then on the right-hand side try to work out how you are going to deal with them. If you don't know, then come back to the problem later, but don't leave the problem unattended for too long once you have acknowledged that it exists.

Don't mislead others

One of the unfortunate knock-on effects of misleading yourself is that you will often end up misleading others as well. In a business context, this may be your customers, suppliers or staff. This may be surmountable in the short term, so long as you rectify it quickly. Far worse, however, is when those close to you are misled. This could be as simple as your friends and family believing you are happy when actually you are not. You could live with that for a while I suppose, although it's not ideal. Unfortunately though, this sort of thing can creep up on you to the point where it becomes quite serious. There have been plenty of cases where the breadwinner fails to tell their partner or dependents that they are not making enough money to cover their outgoings. Sometimes they are losing a fortune, but pride prevents them from mentioning it. The fallout is never good.

You will be rumbled

For anyone reading who has a tendency to exaggerate, be economical with the truth, or worse still, not tell the truth, there is a rude awakening coming: you will be rumbled. We established in Chapter 5 that honesty is crucial to your continued success. Also be wary of fictitious success stories. The world is full of urban myths about how somebody somewhere has made a fortune by doing very little. Very few of them are true. They are a type of fool's gold in their own right.

A positive, realistic attitude can be more effective than the business idea itself. You don't necessarily need massive muscle, intergalactic originality or aggressive behaviour to get on in the world of business. A solid idea, well executed by a positive person will in most cases be more than enough to realize their financial and emotional needs. It all boils down to doing what you can, in a manner that makes you a pleasure to do business with. So keep an eye on frantic behaviour. Stay calm. Don't let the business gain speed without you determining why and whether it is desirable. Just do what you can, in an orderly fashion.

> *"A hero is the one who does what he can."*
>
> **Romain Rolland, quoted in The Times**

Chapter 7 checklist

1. Do not gain speed just for the sake of it.
2. Busier doesn't always mean better.
3. If it's not working, admit it. Don't dig a deeper hole.
4. Predict pitfalls before they happen.
5. Work out when to quit, change direction and move on.
6. Identify your hates, then ditch them.
7. Face up to failure and don't be embarrassed about it.
8. You can't deal with the facts unless you can face them.
9. Use your experience to spot fool's gold.
10. Don't kid yourself, and don't mislead others – you will be rumbled.

Daily Reinvention

This chapter covers how to change your offer every day, week, month or year. The value of one in a row. Rewarding yourself appropriately. Don't get stuck in a rut. Dealing with setbacks: BOHICA. Learning from other people's biggest mistakes and worst disasters. Partners, personalities and personal issues. Money, more customers and moving customers. Technology, timing and trust.

Change your offer every day, week, month or year

The great thing about running your own business is that you can make of it what you want, when you want. This is the bridge to keeping the whole thing fresh. There is no excuse for getting bored when you are the one in charge of what you do all day. That's why it is great fun to change your offer every day, week, month or year – whatever frequency suits the nature of your business. That's a form of daily reinvention that could keep you stimulated by your business for a lifetime.

There are those that maintain that what they do is set in stone, but I don't really believe it. Let's look at some examples of businesses where people say there isn't much room for manoeuvre:

Type of business	Possible changes
Paperclip manufacturer	1. Make them multicoloured 2. Make them from different materials 3. Market them in strange places
Sandwich shop	1. Deliver locally 2. Use exotic ingredients 3. Cater for office events
Garage	1. Offer mobile MOTs 2. Make it as welcoming as a coffee shop 3. Recruit and train female mechanics

There are always those who are happy to tell you that their line of work is mundane, but I never want to agree. There is potential for variety in pretty much everything. As teachers often say, there is no such thing as an uninteresting subject, merely a disinterested student. Daily reinvention helps you to keep this virtuous cycle of freshness on the move.

One in a row

People always like the idea of several successes in a sequence to create the impression of momentum. There's nothing wrong with that, and there is a lot of truth in the old saying that success breeds success. So if you are fortunate enough to be on a roll, then by all means carry on. But most of us aren't that lucky, if indeed luck comes into it. Part of the knack of running your own business is to generate your own confidence, and this can come from the smallest things. We talked earlier in the book about how small things can be brilliant, and this is another example.

You don't have to have loads of triumphs all at the same time, or in a blistering sequence, to find your motivation or to stay motivated. Years ago when I was in charge of new business at an advertising agency, I analysed our success rate at winning new clients versus that of our competitors. The strike rate per year was always about the same – agencies would win about 50% of what they went for. So if you won three out of six in any given year, who cares whether the sequence was *win/lose/win/lose/win/lose* or *win/win/win/lose/lose/lose*? There is no material difference to the volume of work or the income, and yet the three-in-a-row agency would always be the one trumpeting success. But to me, winning one new customer is a reason for celebration in its own right. Hence the expression: one in a row.

One in a row is a little bit of personal philosophy that can be of huge value to the small businessperson. It has two specific elements. First, it captures the moment. A common failing with those who are too busy is that they fail to pause and reflect on their successes as they occur. They're simply too busy to enjoy it, which is a massive shame. After all, what is life for if not enjoying the little things? So use the one-in-a-row idea to register and cherish your little victories. Second, it encapsulates the next step forward. Many people have trouble generating forward motion in their businesses. A one-in-a-row perspective automatically creates the springboard for the next thing along. It is essentially self-feeding, and when it is your own business that really matters.

Making progress gradually is a highly desirable thing. It gives you time to absorb the consequences of the achievement, and make the necessary adjustments to make sure that your business can cope with the new task. An alternative version of the two sequences above could just as easily read *win/cope/win/cope/win/cope and win/win/win/panic/panic/panic*.

Rewarding yourself appropriately

When you do make some progress, it is really important to reward yourself appropriately. The word reward has many connotations, but in this context I mean fairly modest things. I don't mean millions of pounds, luxury yachts or villas in Monte Carlo. I mean small gestures that denote your progress and give you a positive sense of pride in tasks well done. There are lots of different ways of rewarding yourself. Here are some examples:

Achievement	Possible reward
Did what I set out to by 11am	Cappuccino and a Danish
Cleared everything on my checklist	Pint of premium lager
High praise from a customer	Afternoon off to visit art gallery
Won a new contract	Slap-up meal for partner and family
Healthy profit for the year	Chunky dividend

Clearly, the first reward might cost a few quid and the final one many thousands of pounds. That's the whole point. The ability to reward yourself appropriately is a critical part of retaining your sanity when you work for yourself. Many business owners are working so hard that they never even stop to appreciate what they have achieved. This rather defeats the object of setting it up in the first place. Try writing your own list. Start with an achievement column, taking little examples first that crop up frequently in your working day or week. Then move on to more significant monthly or annual milestones. Then dream up some suitable rewards to match each piece of progress. If you like what you have come up with, then put reminders in your diary for the long-term ones. These will turn into pleasant moments somewhere in the future, and play a part in generating a sense of momentum.

Don't get stuck in a rut

Daily reinvention means not getting stuck in a rut. Don't just look for opportunities to do the unexpected – create them. Change as much as is appropriate as often as possible.

Look for ways to be creative all the time. If everything has been the same for ages, then it is down to you to do something about it. Change not only keeps you stimulated, but it is usually good for customers too. You are less likely to be caught on the hop by the competition, and new ideas often capture the imagination of your customers, or help you to attract new ones.

Here's a quick method for stopping your business getting stuck in a rut. Take a piece of paper and write down the main things that your business does. Now have a look at the scoring system in Figure 8.1.

By each area of business, write down a score from one to five. As you can see, the higher the score, the more satisfied you should be. The assumption here is that your enjoyment level will be closely correlated with the sameness of your work and, to a degree, the length of time you have been doing it. It is of course possible that you have been doing the same thing for years and you still love it – in which case, that is fine. More likely though, variety will increase enjoyment. Every now and again ask yourself some searching questions. Is that the same as it has always been? Are you stimulated by it? Are you bored? Always change before your lack of enthusiasm seeps into your working day and becomes apparent to your customers.

---

1. Absolutely hate it
2. Don't enjoy it
3. Boring but tolerable
4. Quite like it
5. Absolutely love it

Fig. 8.1: Stuck in a rut scoring system

Dealing with setbacks: BOHICA

We briefly touched on BOHICA in Chapter 5. It stands for *Bend Over, Here It Comes Again*. This charming concept was introduced to me by my old school friend Richard Wyatt-Haines. Okay, so it's mildly scatological, but it is a very poignant acronym. Small businesses should not have to be at the mercy of larger ones. The way some business owners carry on, you wonder why they allow themselves to be trodden on from a great height so frequently. It all comes down to your personal pride and integrity. If, on reflection, you feel that your business is being too servile, under-charging, over-delivering and generally being too subservient, then it is time to change something. You'll feel so much better when you refuse to take it any more.

Fear often prevents businesses from confronting customers who mistreat them. They think they will lose the business, that they will never replace the income, or that the customer will never change their approach. The outcome is rarely as disastrous as was originally feared, and it is undoubtedly better to die standing up than to live on your knees. Sometimes, bullying customers do listen to comment and try to change their approach. Even if things can't be reconciled and their custom moves on, many businesses find this quite liberating because it allows them to reinvent themselves in another area with other customers. So do not let your business be subjected to BOHICA. Take a deep breath, and don't stand for it.

Biggest mistakes and worst disasters

The penultimate question in the survey was *What was your biggest mistake or worst disaster?* It is from these answers that we can draw superb inspiration from how others have dealt with setbacks. Unlike many corporations who refuse to admit to their mistakes, small business owners are always the first to come clean about their cock-ups. As far as they are concerned, it is all about learning and being human. We all make mistakes, and when we have made enough, they call it experience.

You only have to glance at this section in Appendix II to see that the list of calamities is long, be they self-inflicted or simply being at the mercy of other forces. So I have organized them into three parts, under the banner of an acronym: PMT. Apart from premenstrual tension, it could equally stand for Professional Meltdown Theory, People Mean Trouble or Permanent Money Trauma. You can't stop setbacks happening, but you can learn vast amounts from them, and that is the key to the development of your personality and your business.

Partners, personalities and personal issues

It's funny how all the people issues begin with a P. If this bit isn't right, then you can bet that the business isn't either. People have terrible trouble with their selection of business partner, and dealing with themselves. Let's look at partners first. Lots of people choose to go into business with a partner or partners. Presumably this is because they think they make a good team, or that the other people compensate for skills they don't have. One way or another, thousands do it, and it often goes wrong. The most commonly stated gripes are:

1. Poor choice of partners.
2. Unclear roles.
3. Lack of communication.

It seems extraordinary that potential business partners don't discuss all this before they sign on the dotted line, but often they really don't – or at least not in enough detail. If you are planning such a venture, then it is vital that you do. Look at the example of Anne Esler, who cites her biggest mistake as:

"Not being as clear as we should have been in the early days about the roles of each of the partners. Not having more dissonance amongst the partners – we tended to agree too much on issues and didn't question each other as much as we should have."

In other words, they didn't question each other enough. Whilst this vague state of affairs can trundle along for a while, eventually it all comes to a head. So think ahead, and make it clear what you want. If you can't see the fit, then don't go into business with other people.

On the purely personal front, all sorts of trouble can brew. Business owners talk of almost burning out, not looking after their personal relationships, and all sorts of other problems. This is a highly personal area, and it is not for me to preach. Just pay attention to yourself, and those who care about you, so that the business doesn't take over your life.

Money, more customers and moving customers

Everyone, but everyone, has money troubles. These include, in no particular order, insufficient financial systems, spending beyond their means, not seeking outside investment, under-pricing (and then not being able to raise prices) and not chasing outstanding money quickly enough.

It is as rare as rocking horse dung to find a business that hasn't had problems to do with the money. The trick is to identify them early and do something swiftly. Once you have rectified the problem, you can laugh about it later, or reflect on it ruefully. But make sure that you act swiftly enough to stop the business going under.

When it comes to more customers, there are two main mistakes that businesses make:

1. Not doing enough business development when they are busy.
2. Expending too much time, energy and emotion on tactical new business efforts.

Number one is a common problem but also a cardinal sin.

CARDINAL SIN:
IF YOU ARE DOING NO NEW BUSINESS,
THEN YOU WILL HAVE NO BUSINESS

I can't stress this strongly enough. If I had a pound for every time somebody told me they were too busy to look for any new business, I would be a very rich man. Once you become over dependent on one or two sources of business, you might as well work for a corporation. Allocate separate specific time for meeting potential customers and staying in the swing. It is vital.

Equally though, you shouldn't expend too much effort on scores of little new business leads that are highly time-consuming but very tactical. A typical example of this is companies who draw up no plan of their own and so spend the whole time reacting to inbound enquiries that may or may not suit their needs.

Losing a big or long-standing customer can be a serious blow, but it shouldn't be a surprise, nor should it be the end of your business. Customers move all the time, and the sooner you acknowledge it, the better. This is what Chris Matthews has to say:

"Losing a large client – that was truly awful. It didn't dent our growth, but it reminded us, very, very painfully, that you have to keep working at success, each and every day. Were they right to fire us; had we done wrong? No – we were doing a cracking job, but a new client executive wanted to work with a team familiar to them and so we were out. That happens – but it still hurt."

Sometimes it is simply unavoidable. Other times not, as Steve Greensted very candidly reveals:

"We lost a client because we were too greedy."

Technology, timing and trust

Technology problems are by definition relatively new to the world of small business, but they are no less powerful for that. I winced when I read the two stories below:

"My biggest mistake was not to invest in a proper IT infrastructure from the beginning. I chose a cheaper route and hired a one-man band who set me up with my own back-up server. However he suddenly disappeared off the face of the earth and after 60 days my software on the server crashed as he'd only given me trial software. I lost so much

key information and spent the next few months cursing the guy. IT is so fundamental within any business that you must employ someone you trust entirely." Caroline Kinsey

"The website caused a lot of delay and headaches. I tried and failed with four different suppliers. At that time (2003) it was really hard to find affordable professional designers: one eventually admitted he was a long-distance lorry driver who did coding more or less as a hobby. The next team were two college graduates who were great at design but were defeated by my need for a database in the site. Another company who assured me they could do it were in reality two secondary school teachers working part-time in the evenings. All this caused months of delay and wasted money." Griselda Mussett

Happily both these ladies now run successful businesses, but these were very close calls with technology and I wouldn't like to have been in their shoes. If you can possibly do so, learn from these experiences and don't cut corners in the early days. You may feel that you are saving money but you may well be storing up a disaster for later.

The second T, timing, is represented by two distinctly contrasting ends of a continuum:

1. Not doing it early enough.
2. Rushing too much.

Somewhere in between the two is usually sound advice.

The same applies for the third T, trust. Small business owners struggle somewhere between the extremes of:

1. Not trusting my instincts.
2. Being too trusting and naïve.

The truth is that this is incredibly hard to get right, and near impossible to generalize about. The best I can suggest is to trust your instincts, and to be as sure as you can possibly be if you place your trust in someone else.

Due to tomorrow's weather...

My partner Sarah was sitting on a train from Milton Keynes to London when the steward made an announcement: *"Due to tomorrow's weather, we will only be running a Sunday service..."* This is extraordinary. Think about it. The announcer was assuming that things would be bad tomorrow, and was arranging things accordingly. Imagine if businesses did this? If you assume that tomorrow or next week or next month will be problematic, then chances are they will be. Optimism is a crucial part of your armoury. Pessimism will curtail your business efforts tremendously, often to the point where you become your own worst enemy. Your business will be subjected to enough pressures without you placing extra constraints on it.

The moral of this story for small businesses is not to predict that tomorrow will be poor. If you do, then it probably will be.

A few moments now...

Daily reinvention requires thought and reflection. This need not necessarily take up vast amounts of time, but it does need to be done. How many times have you heard people say that they are so busy that they haven't had time to think? This is not a sustainable state of affairs. You simply must pause and think sometimes. Investing a few moments now will reap superb dividends later, because you will constantly be fine-tuning your approach. This will bring greater purpose to everything you do, and mean that you rarely do things without knowing why. So your sense of achievement and level of satisfaction should remain consistently high.

Should you be in such a perpetual blind panic that you never do take a few moments to reflect and reinvent, then the consequences could be rather unsatisfactory. At minimum, you will fail to enjoy the excellent little moments that your business will undoubtedly create for you. You may well also miss certain opportunities because you were too preoccupied either to spot them or to take advantage of them. But ultimately, failure to reinvent will leave you static while the world moves on, which is undesirable for you and your business.

Are we there yet?

It's a question that children always ask, and one that I devoted a whole chapter to in a previous book – *So What?* The question *Are we there yet?* has two answers:

1. Absolutely. The moment you started investigating your own business, you arrived.
2. Absolutely not. Your work is never finished.

Chapter 8 checklist

1. Change your offer every day, week, month or year.
2. Celebrate individual successes ("one in a row").

3. Reward yourself appropriately.
4. Don't get stuck in a rut.
5. Deal with setbacks rapidly.
6. Learn from other people's biggest mistakes and worst disasters.
7. Pay careful attention to partners, personalities and personal issues.
8. Assume your best customers will move and always look for new ones.
9. Don't skimp on technology.
10. Trust your instincts.

Marketing Matters

This chapter covers why good communication is essential. How much should you spend? Say hello to everyone who could help. Don't be afraid to ask for mini favours. The things you need to know about marketing. Pre-marketing: what it is and why it works. Start-up marketing ideas. Things to reflect on after a few months of marketing. Relaxed selling lines. Escape lines. Why going again is vital.

> *"Never be afraid to tell the world who you are."*
>
> **Anonymous, quoted on Slashdot.org**

Why bother to communicate?

We have looked at how to start from scratch, how to keep the idea pure and not let it be pecked to death by ducks. We have examined the contrast between lifestyle and build-to-sell, along with what that means for the way you set up and run the business. We have discussed the leap of faith needed to get going, the humour, honesty and humility to run it, and the difference between hard and clever work. The last two chapters have covered how not to gain speed at the expense of altitude, and how to reinvent yourself and your business daily. But all of this effort could be irrelevant if you don't bother to tell anybody about it.

The value of communication

There are lots of businesses that do not bother with marketing. They leave communication to chance. Is this a good thing? Who cares if your business communicates well? Does it have any bearing on your fortunes? Can you live without marketing? Most companies wrestle with these issues at some point in their development.

> *"Failure to communicate creates a vacuum which is usually filled by misinformation, drivel and poison."*
>
> **C. Northcote Parkinson**

What happens if you choose not to communicate adequately? Nothing disastrous, you might reasonably conclude. However, as your business grows, so will its reputation, and a reputation is a fragile bundle of opinions that could have a significant bearing on your success. The problem is that, if you decide to say nothing, customers will simply draw their own conclusions. Their view may be accurate and well informed, but then again it might not.

> *"Whether you like it or not, you will have a reputation, so you might as well have a bearing on what it is."*
>
> **Anon**

Your business is going to develop a reputation whether you like it or not. Every business does. In the early days, this may be narrow in scope, but eventually it develops into a fairly complex set of opinions, possibly held by lots of groups of your customers, based on various layers of interaction and experience. So it exists whether you want it to or not. Put simply, your reputation is determined by:

- How you behave personally.
- How you tell people you behave.
- How you tell your people to behave (if you have them).

It all starts with you. You need to tell anyone who will listen what type of business you are. That's half the battle. Then tell your staff (if you have them). They need to behave in a way that is appropriate to what you stand for, and what you believe to be right. They can only do this if they are told what is expected of them. And of course you need to behave that way yourself.

How much should you spend?

Much has been written about appropriate marketing investment levels. As a rough rule of thumb, mature companies that embrace marketing as a discipline spend 8–13% of their turnover on it. They don't do this for fun, but for hard-nosed commercial reasons that have been proven to improve their fortunes. Most modern companies have concluded that there is essentially no difference between marketing and sales. As such, they believe that to have "no marketing" is to abdicate from sales altogether.

The answer for small businesses may be quite different. There is a huge difference between paid-for marketing and free marketing. Your most powerful weapon in the early days is you. You need to get out and about and promote what you do vigorously. Remind yourself of the proposition you invented in Chapter 2. Practice saying it, and get good at it. So to start with, you may not have to spend any money on marketing at all. How can that be done?

Say hello to everyone who could help

It is extraordinary the number of people who haven't even bothered to let everyone know what they do for a living. This is one of the most powerful forms of marketing, and yet many leave it out completely. Word of mouth is free, and much more persuasive than any marketing you might pay for. Everybody you meet is a potential customer, but that isn't the main point. Far more important is the fact that, even if they don't want what you have to offer, they might know someone who does. Creating a buzz around what you do is a phenomenon that has been written about a great deal. *Buzz*, a book by Salzman, Matathia and O'Reilly, says that everyone has a different definition of it, but roughly it has to be organic, centred on conversations, peer driven and spreading outwards from the original discoverers. The thing consumers trust most these days is personal experience, so try to harness it for the benefit of your business. There is a summary of the book in Appendix I. So say hello to everyone – they might just turn out to be a customer or, better still, an ambassador for what you do.

Don't be afraid to ask for mini favours

The same goes for when you need a bit of help in the early days. Don't be afraid to ask for mini favours from people to get you going. This applies to marketing as much as to painting the walls of your first office or shop. Do you have any contacts that could help spread the word about what you do? Would they mind if you promoted your business on their premises? Think broadly about the possibilities – the chances are, they will say yes. And don't forget to return the favour when they need one from you.

The only ten things you need to know about marketing

1. Marketing is not complicated.
2. Marketing doesn't have to take long.

3. Marketing doesn't have to cost much. It can even be free.
4. You can write your approach on the back of a napkin and be enacting it next week.
5. Marketing isn't a panacea, but if you don't let people know what you are offering you might as well be sitting in a mud hut with the world's best kept secret.
6. People actually like paying a lot for products and services, so long as they are high quality and you give them a reason to justify it.
7. Strategy is just a posh word for describing what you have decided to do.
8. All your staff have a role to play in marketing, every time they talk to anyone outside the company.
9. In tough times, ignore the 80:20 rule. Instead, just market hard to your top 1%. You will save time, and keep your margin.
10. Brave marketing decisions tend to reap larger rewards than safe ones.

Pre-marketing

One of the most frequent problems with marketing is that people leave it far too late. Of course it depends on the nature of what your business is selling, but often people need time to think about what they might need from you. They won't just make a snap decision based on 30 seconds of chat from you. If you can acknowledge this early on, then you can build that consideration time into your plan. Impulse purchases are fine, but higher-value items need thought.

So by pre-marketing, I mean letting people know what you can do for them, or provide them with, long before you actually want their custom. In the early days you may find this difficult because you want the sale quickly, but it doesn't take long for you to be building a pipeline of interest that could materialize at some later point in the future. Start this process now, and your efforts will be less desperate later.

Some start-up marketing ideas

> *"A stand can be made against invasion by an army; no stand can be made against invasion by an idea."*
>
> **Victor Hugo, quoted in The Independent**

1. Start with the basics. Think about what you actually want to achieve and define your objectives clearly. Make sure you seek out the right people in the right way to get the best results. It is important to listen to your customers and their needs to ensure that your product or service really satisfies their requirements.

2. Get connected. Consider placing your business in a directory such as the Yellow Pages, local business directories such as the Chamber of Commerce or local web directories. It may seem obvious, but with a one-off payment each year you can reach anyone who is directly looking for your product or service.

3. DIY public relations. PR is a good way of getting free publicity. Write your own press releases in the manner of a news story and send it to your local papers and business magazines.

4. Be creative. Creative services do not have to cost a fortune. Agencies that specialize in working with small businesses are often flexible and good value. Try sharing costs and creative ideas with other local firms who are in a similar situation.

5. Improve your website. Constructing a website can cost as little as a few hundred pounds but is a vital marketing tool. Customers now expect to see a website as much as they do a brochure. Bear in mind that a bad or out-of-date website is as bad as none at all.

6. Keep in touch. Newsletters and emails are a very effective way of reminding your customers of your presence, as well as giving you the chance to promote new products or pass on news about your business. However, only contact those by email who have specifically given you permission.

7. Encourage word of mouth. Offer your existing customers incentives to recommend you to others. Send out a referral form with each delivery or invoice, making it as easy as possible for your customers to do so. Also include testimonials from existing customers on your website and business literature.

8. Try something new. The Internet is a good resource for marketing, but you have to make your business stand out. Try using a pay-per-click service on a search engine. Each click can cost as little as a few pence.

9. Show off. Trade exhibitions provide an ideal place to meet your customers and potential clients face to face, and usually give you a chance to check out the competition. Looking at what works and what doesn't for others can help you avoid making expensive mistakes yourself.

10. Learn from your past. Analyse which marketing efforts were effective and which were not, and ask yourself why, in order to refine and improve next year's marketing.

Some things to reflect on after a few months of marketing

The old joke goes that when a marketing campaign hasn't worked, the immediate reaction of most companies is to do some more. This doesn't make much sense. You'd be better off having a careful think about why things happened as they did. Here are some questions you might want to ask after you have tried a few things:

- Is the original approach still relevant? (If not, change it)
- Is the meeting mix right? (Duration, frequency, content)
- Have you got the right staff and the right blend of delegation and decision-making?
- Are your suppliers performing well? (If not, is it you or them?)
- Have you reviewed all the marketing materials recently?
- Have you come up with any new ideas recently?
- Do you have a reporting system that works well?
- Do you get the information you want when you need it?
- What is morale like and, if it is bad, what ideas are there to improve it?

Learn from your experiences. Make changes. And try to do something unexpected in the next few weeks.

Relaxed selling lines

Some people have terrible trouble chatting at social occasions, particularly about their business. And yet these are some of the best opportunities to spread the word about what you do. Here are four questions to set you off:

1. What's the big issue at your company at the moment?
2. What's your main personal objective at the moment?
3. What's your favourite hobby?
4. Do you have a partner or kids?

Once they have answered, you can develop the conversation along the following lines:

- Is there anything in particular that you feel strongly about?
- Is that something we could help you with?
- Would you like a meeting in the next couple of weeks to discuss it?
- Do you have a card on you and may I get in touch?

It's simple enough stuff. You only need a couple of ideas up your sleeve to get chatting and see if there might be possible business at the end of it.

Escape lines

There will of course be occasions when you can't get away from someone in a social situation. If that's the case, try these:

1. Will you excuse me for a moment? I need to go to the loo.
2. Can I introduce you to a friend?
3. Do you mind if I circulate? I'm rather on duty tonight.
4. Will you excuse me? I need to have a quick word with Steve.
5. Someone has just caught my eye and I am being summoned. I'll be back in a moment. (Strangely, you never return)

Go again

> *"You'll always have the chance to give up, so why do it now?"*
>
> **Anon**

To summarize, marketing is simply the regular explanation of what you do to anyone who will listen. It can be free, and if you can keep it that way, then so much the better. Keep going again and again with new ideas. There is no point in your business being beautifully run on the one hand and the world's best kept secret on the other. Spread the word. Let the world know.

Chapter 9 checklist

1. Good communication is essential to the health of your business.
2. You may not need to spend any money to have an effect.
3. Say hello to everyone who could help.
4. Don't be afraid to ask for mini favours.
5. The things you need to know about marketing are actually quite straightforward.
6. Pre-marketing is essential to avoid short-term desperate marketing.
7. Try some start-up marketing ideas to start with.
8. Reflect for a while after a few months of marketing.
9. Use relaxed selling lines in social situations.
10. Always go again – persistence is vital

This chapter draws together what they all say about starting your business. Self-motivation. Money. Action. Relationships. Toughness. Chinese whispers. The invisible support network. You choose this life. And your duty to pass that knowledge on when you have been there yourself.

What they all say

And so we reach the end of our journey. You may have rushed out and started your business already, or you may still be pondering. Either way, there is one fascinating thing left to do, and that is to sweep up all the brilliant wisdom from those who have already been there. To extract these gems, I asked everybody: *What's the one piece of advice you would pass on?* What emerged was a manifesto to inspire you even in the worst of times. The subject matter is broad-ranging and covers almost every aspect of life, so I have organized it into a SMART plan: Self-motivation, Money, Action, Relationships, Toughness.

Self-motivation

To start and run your own business, it is essential that you believe in yourself. You've got to go for it and not give a stuff what other people say. As Tom Helliwell says:

"Don't listen to the non-believers that are working for 'institutions' who tell you 'you will fail'. If you work hard and focus on most of the right areas you will succeed."

Develop successful habits as best you can. Ditch the type of behaviour that doesn't get you anywhere. Do it because you love it, not for the cash. The cash will follow if you trust your instincts. Honestly, everyone says it. Develop a positive attitude. As Gordon Haxton says:

"Don't look for negatives."

Never become complacent. Running your own business is a life's work, needing constant attention.

Money

Don't under-price – you will regret it later. Don't over-deliver – your customers will think it is normal and expect it every time. Be as tough on financial matters as you can. As Giles Fraser says:

"Don't be shy to be tough on financial Terms and Conditions, and stick to them."

Remember that what you know is valuable. Do not give your time and advice away for nothing. Never expect payment on time. You need to build significant time lags into your plans so that you don't go bust. As a piece of life philosophy, don't do it for the money. Do it so you can spend every day doing something you love.

Action

Plan your exit from day one, as recommended in Chapter 3. Don't go for perfection – try things out in rough form. Never stop business development, even when you are frantically busy – you will end up with a big hole in the business at some point later. Keep your marketing ideas and materials up to date, and keep it fresh with new thinking. As Andy Tilley says:

"Commercial Darwinism is a continual requirement so take some risks and don't polish turds. Too much time is spent trying to get things perfect when you need to try them out in imperfect form."

Be prepared to change your plan constantly and take advantage of new opportunities when they happen. Learn as you go along. Remember that the more you put in, the more you get out.

Relationships

Build your network before you start. This will provide excellent moral support as well as potential business. Network non-stop – this is a job that should never be finished. Running your own business is as much about relationships as it is about content or product. Concentrate hard on communication, particularly with partners. As Paul Flynn says:

"Talk! Don't bottle up grievances. It will only make them worse."

Leave your ego at home – no one else is interested. Look for the best in people. Treat everyone with the same respect and smile. Guard against becoming too dependent on one client, particularly if you have become good mates with them. Consider getting a mentor or coach – they can provide a calm word and a different perspective when you need it.

Toughness

Have a five-year plan and stick to it. Or choose a suitable time span for your line of business. Be prepared to take calculated risks – if you don't take any at all then nothing much will happen and you will become frustrated. Develop a resilient streak. As Sheila Gimson says:

"Get back up fighting when you are knocked down."

Accept that things won't always work, and don't be afraid to kill them off and move on.

Chinese whispers

As you move from considering starting your business, to actually doing so, to learning a lot, it gradually becomes your job to pass on your wisdom, just as the people in this book have done. This form of Chinese whispers is critical to the vitality of all small businesses, and you can play your part.

The invisible support network

Help people out, and they will help you out. Pay it forward. Don't be afraid to make mistakes. Just rectify things quickly when they go wrong. That's how we learn, and build experience.

> *"A stumble may prevent a fall."*
>
> **Thomas Fuller, quoted in The Independent**

You choose this life

Never forget, you choose what to do in this life, and if you choose to start your own business then it is your responsibility to make it a success, and pass that knowledge on to others. The rewards are exceptional, particularly the emotional ones. Good luck, and if you haven't already, now would be a good time to *Start*.

APPENDICES

Appendix I: Book Summaries

BOOK: *Buzz*
AUTHORS: Marian Salzman, Ira Matathia,
Ann O'Reilly

What the book says

- Everyone has a different definition of buzz, but roughly it has to be organic, centred on conversational value, peer driven and spread outwards from trend setters to trend spreaders and on to the mainstream.
- The only thing consumers trust these days is personal experience.
- Word of mouth (WOM) should be renamed WORM because of the way it insinuates itself into the conscious.
- There is a Buzz Continuum which runs from the lunatic fringe (2%), to the Alphas (8%), to the Bees (20%), to the mainstream (50%), to the laggards (20%).
- Much of buzz marketing lies in the critical zone between "best kept secret" and "everyone's doing it".

What's good about it

- It is probably worth trying to explain and categorize a phenomenon which plays a large part in modern marketing but is quite hard to describe.
- Media saturation is nicely summarized: "A single weekday edition of the New York Times contains more data than a typical c.17 citizen of England would have encountered in a lifetime."
- It acknowledges the similarity to the Tipping Point book and tries to build on it by explaining the role of superconnectors and by adding a degree of quantification and case history work to the concept.
- It offers four springboards to generate buzz:
  1. *Cultivate a culture of creativity.*
  2. *Give 'em (consumers) what they always wanted.*
  3. *Capture the moment.*
  4. *Challenge the conventions.*
- It is honest enough to include advice on how to handle negative buzz as well as generate the positive – a form of crisis management.

What you have to watch

- The thinking is not particularly original. It is very much a reorganization of lots of other recent work that covers influencers, tipping points and how to seed trends in influential minorities in order to ignite mass acceptance.
- It is written by people who work for Euro RSCG, so it is rather self-congratulatory and from time to time strays into the realm of credentials.

BOOK: ***The Economist Guide to Management Ideas***

AUTHOR: **Tim Hindle**

What the book says

- A two-page synopsis of all the important management ideas:

Activity-based costing	Balanced scorecard	Barriers to entry and exit
Benchmarking	Brainstorming	Branding
Business cycle	Business modelling	The business plan
Cannibalisation	Championing	Change management
Cherry-picking	Clustering	Competitive advantage
Convergence	Core competence	Corporate governance
Corporate social responsibility	Cost–benefit analysis	Crisis management
Critical path analysis	Cross-selling	Culture
Customer relationship management	Decentralisation	Delayering
Differentiation	Diversification	Double-loop learning
Downsizing	e-Commerce	Economies of scale
Economies of scope	Empowerment	Enterprise resource planning

Entrepreneurship	Excellence	The experience curve
Family firms	Franchising	Game theory
The glass ceiling	Globalisation	Growth share matrix
The Hawthorne effect	Hierarchy of needs	Innovation
Intrapreneurship	Just-in-time	Kaizen
Keiretsu	Knowledge management	Leadership
Lean production	The learning organisation	Management by objectives
Management by walking about	Mass customisation	Mass production
Matrix management	Mentoring	Mission statement
Niche market	Open-book management	Operational research
Outsourcing	The Pareto principle (80/20)	Performance-related pay
The Peter principle	Planned obsolescence	Portfolio working
Post-merger integration	Process improvement	Product life-cycle
Quality circle	Re-engineering	Satisficing
Scenario planning	Scientific management	Segmentation
The Seven Ss	Six sigma	Small is beautiful
Span of control	Strategic alliance	Strategic planning
Structure	Succession planning	SWOT analysis
Synergy	Technology transfer	Theories X and Y
Total quality management	True and fair	Unbundling

Unique selling proposition	Value chain	Value creation
Vertical integration	The virtual organisation	Vision
Zero-based budgeting		

Some less well-known examples

Double-loop learning: How learning organizations amend their practices on the go.

The Hawthorne effect: The performance of workers is influenced by their surroundings.

Kaizen: Continuous improvement involving everyone, managers and workers alike.

Keiretsu: Headless combine in which several companies form a truly equal joint venture.

The Peter principle: In a hierarchy, every employee rises to their level of incompetence.

Satisficing: Individuals will make do with what is satisfactory.

Six sigma: In quality management perfection is unrealistic, so near-perfection will do.

The Seven Ss: Strategy, structure, systems, skills, shared values, staff, style.

BOOK: *Getting Things Done*
AUTHOR: David Allen

What the book says

- It is possible for a person to have an overwhelming number of things to do and still function productively with a clear head and a positive sense of relaxed control.
- You should only have one filing system.
- You should turn your in-tray upside down and work on the principle of First In First Out (FIFO), not LIFO as many people do.
- It's a five-stage system: collect, process, organize, review, do.
- Do it, delegate it, or defer it.
- Nothing should take more than two minutes, nor go back into your in-tray.
- The four crucial factors are context, time, energy and priority.
- There is a six-level model for reviewing your work, using an aerospace analogy: 50,000+ feet, life; 40,000 feet, three- to five-year vision; 30,000 feet, one- to two-year goals; 20,000 feet, areas of responsibility; 10,000 feet, current projects; runway, current actions.

What's good about it

- If you have problems being organized and getting things done, this book will sort you out.
- The more relaxed you are, the more effective you will be (as in karate). Applied to all parts of your life, and

not necessarily the most urgent bits, this becomes Black Belt Management.

- You have to concentrate on the very next physical action required to move the situation forward. There are lots of good quotes:

"This constant preoccupation with all the things we have to do is the single largest consumer of time and energy."

"Blessed are the flexible, for they shall not be bent out of shape."

"Everything should be made as simple as possible, but not simpler."

"I am rather like a mosquito in a nudist camp. I know what I want to do, but I don't know where to begin."

"The middle of every project looks like a disaster."

"Talk does not cook rice."

"There are risks and costs to a program of action, but they are far less than the long-range costs of comfortable inaction."

What you have to watch

- Nothing. This is an international bestseller and it works.

BOOK: ***Hello Laziness***
AUTHOR: **Corinne Maier**

What the book says

- This is an unusual book that provides a counterpoint to all those that suggest that increasing productivity is the key to success.
- It says that you can be a slacker and get away with it, and that only by reducing your productivity to zero do you have any chance of climbing the corporate ladder.
- Hard work and long hours won't get you anywhere.
- Companies don't care. They hate individuals who don't conform.
- They talk gibberish, use people as pawns, and move them around so no one can keep track.
- They have no ethics, no culture, and have mastered the art of appearing more intelligent than they actually are.

What's good about it

- It's good to take the opposite view from time to time, if only to test what you believe.
- There are typologies of idiots: Mr Average, The Hollow Man(ager), Consultants who con, Timewasters, Yes-Men and Nobodies.
- The idea that business is effectively doomed is an intriguing one.
- What is a job for? Many workers genuinely don't know what they are paid for, so why should they fear being lazy?
- The author's ten new commandments of work are:
  1. Salaried work is the new slavery.

2. It's pointless trying to change the system.
3. The work you do is fundamentally pointless.
4. You'll be judged on your ability to conform, not your work.
5. Never accept positions of responsibility.
6. Seek out the most useless jobs.
7. Hide away and stay there.
8. Learn how to read the subtle cues that tell you who else has rumbled all this.
9. Temporary staff do all the work – treat them well.
10. Business ideology is no more "true" than communism.

What you have to watch

- It is translated from the French and reflects many of the strange working practices in corporate France.
- If you choose to enact a large proportion of this book, you may get fired.

BOOK: *How To Be A Complete And Utter Failure ...*

AUTHOR: **Steve McDermott**

What the book says

- The full title is How To Be A Complete And Utter Failure In Life, *Work And Everything* (subtitled *39-and-a-half steps to lasting underachievement*).
- Do the opposite of everything in this book and you'll be a great success.
- The steps include:
  Don't decide what you want.
  Don't do things on purpose.
  Don't know what you value in life.
  Don't put your goals in writing.
  Don't plan your priorities.
  Don't have a mentor.
  Don't take action right now.
  Don't get feedback.
  Don't adjust.
  Don't practice continuous improvement.
  Don't expand your comfort zone.
  Don't ask "How do you do that?"
  Don't commit to lifelong learning.

What's good about it

- If you are looking for ways of improving what you do, this a good compendium.
- It uses a light-hearted format to remind you of lots of methods that will help, and bad habits that don't.

What you have to watch

- The back-to-front language (do the opposite of everything that is suggested) becomes a bit tortuous at times, and the joke wears a bit thin when repeated throughout a whole book.
- There is no contents, index, bibliography or references, so it is almost impossible to find anything a second time without skimming the whole book.

BOOK: *How Not To Come Second*
AUTHOR: David Kean

What the book says

- This book is subtitled *The Art of Winning Business Pitches*.
- The author used to work at Lowe, DDB and Omnicom.
- It constantly returns to the point that it is all about the winning. Far too many pitches fail because people don't do the simple things and get distracted.
- Elements of getting it wrong include: deluding yourself that you were a very close second; trying to over-complicate things that are actually simple; and people who are professionals most of the time acting like amateurs in the pitch process.

What's good about it

- Although it's all obvious stuff, clients want a good team, people who understand them and their business, some fun and stimulation, good value and problem solving. There is many a pitch that does not deliver these.
- The ingredients for successful pitching are:
  1. Be organized.
  2. Know your audience (many agencies pitch blind).
  3. Solve the problem.
  4. Price properly (note – not "cheaply").
  5. Practice (methodically, not at the last minute).
  6. Great presentations.
  7. Unstoppable momentum.
  8. Feedback.

- Other advice includes compiling the pitch bible, meeting every day, brainstorming with the top talent, networking like crazy and having a mole on the client side.
- It identifies four types (*expressives, amiables, drivers, analyticals*) who may be present on your team and the client side. They require careful casting.
- Pitch on a postcard is a good idea – if you can't fit your argument on one, it's not good enough.

What you have to watch

- The author is English but the book has been adapted for an American audience.
- It briefly falls back on De Bono's Six-Hat Thinking, which isn't new.

BOOK: *Juicing The Orange*
AUTHOR: **Pat Fallon & Fred Senn**

What the book says

- It is subtitled *How to turn creativity into a powerful business advantage.*
- Most leaders have more creativity in their organizations than they realize.
- Identify one critical business problem that needs solving and then rigorously unearth insights that lead to a spectacular solution.
- There are Seven Principles of Creative Leverage:
  1. Always start from scratch.
  2. Demand a ruthlessly simple definition of the business problem.
  3. Discover a proprietary emotion.
  4. Focus on the size of the idea, not the size of the budget.
  5. Seek out strategic risks.
  6. Collaborate or perish.
  7. Listen hard to your customers (then listen some more).

What's good about it

- Starting from scratch is harder said than done, and more marketers should do it, or at least investigate doing it.
- The principles at the heart of the book will resonate with anyone involved in any form of creative marketing:
  1. Creativity will be an increasingly essential business tool.
  2. You can't buy creativity, but you can unlock it.

3. Creativity is not an easy path to walk but the rewards are worth it.
- There are some good case histories from Skoda, Citibank United Airlines and Lee Jeans.

What you have to watch

- The authors are the founders of Fallon so at times the book can read like an agency brochure.
- The seven principles aren't that original or earth-shattering – a helpful reminder of good practice, but not stunningly new in any particular sense.
- American case histories such as Holiday Inn, EDS and Bahamas Ministry of Tourism may be of less interest to UK readers.

BOOK: *Liar's Paradise*
AUTHORS: Graham Edmonds

What the book says

- 80% of companies think that they are fraud free, but a recent survey actually revealed fraud in 45% of them.
- There are seven degrees of deceit:
  1. **White lie:** told to make someone feel better or to avoid embarrassment.
  2. **Fib:** relatively insignificant, such as excuses and exaggerations.
  3. **Blatant:** whoppers used when covering up mistakes or apportioning blame.
  4. **Bullshit:** a mixture of those above combined with spin and bluff to give the best impression.
  5. **Political:** similar to bullshit but with much bigger scale and profile.
  6. **Criminal:** illegal acts from fraud to murder, and their subsequent denial.
  7. **Ultimate:** so large that it must be true. As Joseph Goebbels said: "If you tell a lie big enough and keep repeating it, people will eventually come to believe it."

What's good about it

- It confirms what we all suspect – that the workplace constantly bombards us with lies, fakery and spin.
- Case histories of Enron, Boo.com, the European Union and others provide the proof on a grand scale.
- Deconstructions of other levels of lying help the reader to navigate their way through the day-to-day types. You can then decide how to react.

- It has tips on how to suck up to the boss, pass the buck and endure meetings.
- Everybody should read the chapter on Lies and Leadership.

"The truth is more important than the facts." Frank Lloyd Wright

"Those that think it is permissible to tell white lies soon grow colour blind." Austin O'Malley

"Honesty may be the best policy, but it's important to remember that apparently, by elimination, dishonesty is the second-best policy." George Carlin

What you have to watch

- The book essentially condemns most corporate cultures and so needs to be viewed lightly by those who have to work in them.
- There is a moral dilemma lurking within: do you tell the truth and get trod on, or join the liars?

BOOK: *Screw It, Let's Do It*
AUTHOR: **Richard Branson**

What the book says

- Simple truths in life, and the right attitude, can inspire and enable you to do practically anything.
- People will always try to talk you out of ideas and say "It can't be done", but if you have faith in yourself, it almost always can.

What's good about it

- You can read it in a couple of hours.
- The author has made plenty of mistakes and taken a lot of risks, so this is not just a "plain sailing" manual.
- The main principles of just do it, have fun, be bold, challenge yourself and live the moment are all solid, inspirational stuff.
- There are also much softer elements such as value family and friends, have respect for people and do some good for others.
- You can dip in anywhere and grab a motivational thought in ten seconds.
- Choose from:
  - ~ *Believe it can be done.*
  - ~ *Never give up.*
  - ~ *Have faith in yourself.*
  - ~ *When it's not fun, move on.*
  - ~ *Have no regrets.*
  - ~ *Keep your word.*
  - ~ *Aim high.*

~ Try new things.
~ Love life and live it to the full.
~ Chase your dreams but live in the real world.
~ Face problems head on.
~ Money is for making the right things happen.
~ Make a difference and help others.

What you have to watch

- The book is not particularly well written (the author struggled with mild dyslexia at school), so this is more a stream of consciousness, or a selection of sound bites.
- It always seems easier for someone who has "done it" to reflect back on the hard times – but it is harder to apply that philosophy when you are actually struggling

BOOK: *See, Feel, Think, Do*
AUTHOR: **Andy Milligan & Shaun Smith**

What the book says

- Instinct is much more powerful in business than over-reliance on research or data, which can only provide you with a rear-view mirror picture.
- Focus groups and MBA models are not as good as human instinct or a passion to make a difference.
- By watching and empathizing with real customers and how they act, we can evolve better ideas that solve their real needs.
- *See, Feel, Think, Do* sums up how these intuitive ideas come to fruition.
- Why? is a powerful question and is not asked often enough in business.

What's good about it

See: Experience it for yourself.
What is the current customer experience like? What do they value (or not)?
Feel: Empathizing with your customers.
How do I feel about the experience? How do customers and employees feel? What do they like/dislike?
Think: There is no such thing as a stupid idea.
Why do we do it this way? How could it be better? Why can't we do it?
Do: Make it so.
What changes are needed to people, processes and products? How do we get our people and customers excited about it?

- This is a perfectly sound method that you can apply to any business to see what needs to be changed.
- There are scores of case histories to show how it all works (or doesn't): Carphone Warehouse, Apple iPod, Sony, Heinz, Harley Davidson, First Direct, Barclays, Geek Squad, Cathay Pacific, TNT, and more.

What you have to watch

- The *Think* premise that there is no such thing as a bad idea isn't right. There are clearly lots of bad ideas around.
- Whilst the process provides a framework, it isn't that remarkable. Good business people should be doing this instinctively anyway.

BOOK: ***Simply Brilliant***
AUTHOR: **Fergus O'Connell**

What the book says

- The best ideas aren't always complicated and the incredibly straightforward stuff is often overlooked in the search for a complex answer.
- Many smart people lack the set of essential skills which could roughly be described as "common sense".
- There are seven principles here that can be adapted for attacking most everyday problems:
  1. Many things are simple – *despite our tendency to complicate them.*
  2. You need to know what you're trying to do – *many don't.*
  3. There is always a sequence of events – *make the journey in your head.*
  4. Things don't get done if people don't do them – *strategic wafflers beware!*
  5. Things rarely turn out as expected – *so plan for the unexpected.*
  6. Things either are or they aren't – *don't fudge things.*
  7. Look at things from other's point of view – *it will help your expectations.*

What's good about it

- In a world of over-complication, asking some simple questions can really make your life easier. For example:
  - ~ *What would be the simplest thing to do here?*
  - ~ *Describing an issue or a solution in less than 25 words.*

~ *Telling it as though you were telling a six-year-old.*
~ *Asking whether there is a simpler way.*
- Try writing the minutes of a meeting before the meeting – then you'll know what you want to get out of it.
- It highlights the difference between duration and effort. *"How long will it take you to have a look at that?" "About an hour."* But when?
- It explains the reasons why things don't get done: confusion, over-commitment, inability – usually busy people never say there's a problem!
- Plan your time assuming you will have interruptions – the *"hot date"* scenario.

What you have to watch

- The orientation is very much based on a project management perspective, which is fine if you are one, but others may prefer to cherry-pick the most applicable ideas.
- Anyone who flies by the seat of their pants would have to be very disciplined to apply these ideas. It's a bit like dieting.

Appendix II: Survey responses

The survey

1. *What made you start your own business?*
2. *What was the hardest thing about starting?*
3. *What has been the best thing about it?*
4. *What was your biggest mistake or worst disaster?*
5. *What's the one piece of advice you would pass on?*

Robert Ashton

Business: marketing agency
Employees: 10
Years: 6 (then sold it)

1. What made you start?
Desire for total control of destiny, mounting concern at differing opinions of business partner, school fees!

2. Hardest thing
Balancing the ethics of poaching customers from old firm with the need to eat.

3. Best thing
Buying a derelict farm to create a home for the business and my family.

4. Biggest mistake
Lack of focus and desire to constantly innovate for innovation's sake – now doing just that as a freelance, which is much, much easier.

5. Advice
Look on starting a business as a step in your career, not the rest of your career. It's both inevitable and natural that you will outgrow your business or it will outgrow you – both mean you need to move on... plan for exit from day one.

Steve Barber

Business: printing
Employees: 7
Years: 4

1. What made you start?
I was fed up with earning other people lots of money and only earning a wage, plus I had learnt about the whole business and not just one section I was working in.

2. Hardest thing
Knowing the working side of a business is one thing, but having to sort out the financial and business side is another. But after a while it becomes second nature.

3. Best thing
Seeing the turnover go up... year on year. Seeing the hard work pay off, and at 37 seeing my mortgage pay off within the next 3 years.

4. Biggest mistake
Not had any disasters, but had a few employee mistakes.

5. Advice
Treat everyone with the same respect, and smile.

Renee Botham

Business: business growth specialist
Employees: 19
Years: 18

1. What made you start?
The thought of giving up the business life after having my first child was appealing for about a week!

2. Hardest thing
Nothing. I'm determined, love what I do and just knew that I am good at what I do.

3. Best thing
Seeing our clients win new business, seeing my staff fulfilled. Oh, and paying the bills.

4. Biggest mistake
Not having the confidence to charge at realistic levels and then having to make the decision to hike our rates or decide that we couldn't keep working at the level we were charging. In the end it was a mix of both for survival.

5. Advice
You can't be good at everything, so surround yourself with talented people. God only gave us so many hours in a day – go above that capacity and you will provide

mediocrity, so use people you trust. You employed them and are paying them after all.

Sue Buckle

Business: coach and career consultant
Employees: me
Years: in current format, 3

1. What made you start?
Fed up with other people making decisions about my career and role. This was when it was decided to merge me with another company, and I went from shareholder to non-shareholder for no reason, and with no input into the decision.

2. Hardest thing
Finding the confidence to go it alone, taking on a lease on a London office with no track record.

3. Best thing
Being my own boss, being accountable and responsible, and really understanding how important it is to work cleverly instead of putting in hours for the sake of it. That's three things but they sort of all meld into one, I think.

4. Biggest mistake
Employing someone who was a bad fit – not very clever for a recruitment consultant!

5. Advice
Trust yourself and go for it – you are more likely to regret something you haven't done than something you have.

Andrew Butcher

Business: public relations
Employees: 4, plus freelance
Years: 10 prior to merger with like-minded firm

1. What made you start?
Combination of escape from having a boss who I did not respect and the frustration of knowing that I could make as much or more money, giving clients more of what they wanted and needed, for lower fees – i.e. cutting out the corporate profit drain.

2. Hardest thing
There was nothing hard about starting. It felt like a marvellous release. So the hardest thing is actually recognising that all the negative advice you get from salaried colleagues about insecurity and how brave one is, is all nonsense.

3. Best thing
Not having a boss, taking all of the decisions, not playing politics and delivering the promises you set out to deliver to clients and myself.

4. Biggest mistake
An error in the VAT return, discovered in an inspection on Christmas Eve, leading to a very expensive Christmas for all the wrong reasons.

5. Advice
Surround yourself with the besWWt people – staff and advisers – knowing that you can then trust them to deliver for you. In other words, do not skimp – pay for good people, recognising that to get the best out of them you have to trust them to work without continual checking,

so they need to be good in the first place – setting high standards means either doing it all yourself (hopeless for long term growth) or buying in the best support and making them part of your team.

Paula Carter

Business: communications consultancy
Employees: 1
Years: 7

1. What made you start?
Wanted more flexibility over type of work/location/hours to accommodate family.

2. Hardest thing
Sorting out VAT status – distinct lack of advice!

3. Best thing
Variety and flexibility.

4. Biggest mistake
Charging a low rate to get a job, then not being able to increase rate on next job with same client.

5. Advice
Network, network and network.

Will Collin

Business: marketing services
Employees: 160 across eight offices
Years: 7

1. What made you start?
An ever-present sense that the existing industry was built the wrong way and nobody else seemed to be interested in changing it.

2. Hardest thing
At the very beginning we were vague about what exactly it was that the company did. The temptation is not to close off any potential opportunities by putting yourself in a box. As a result our early presentations were probably a bit confusing – trying to be all things to all people.

3. Best thing
If being an employee is like being in a well-upholstered limousine, running a business is like driving a go-kart. Everything feels faster, and you sense every little bump in the road. The highs feel higher while the lows feel lower. There's always something interesting happening, both good and bad.

4. Biggest mistake
Commercial incontinence – too many commercial side ventures that seemed to make sense in the short term but which ultimately demanded management attention way out of proportion to their likely financial return.

5. Advice
Be lucky.

Chris Cowpe

Business: strategic and marketing advice for companies who want to grow faster
Employees: 3 partners
Years: 2 months

1. What made you start?
Meeting two others who seemed to share my outlook and professional interests: a belief that we had a lot of valuable experience to offer (at a time when there seems little experience around); a belief that clients would value a "short, sharp shock" approach rather than long-winded, process-driven, documented overkill.

2. Hardest thing
Getting partner commitment – we weren't arguing at all, but (and mainly due to their previous work commitments) it seemed to take for ever.

3. Best thing
To be up and running; the first cheque; a belief (albeit with every finger crossed) that we do have something of value; showing my kids the letterhead, etc.

4. Biggest mistake
Not getting IT properly sorted from day one.

5. Advice
See mistake!

Vanessa Dalton

Business: creative services consultancy
Employees: 0
Years: 7 months

1. What made you start?
I had been working for the same company for 7 years and had reached a position that enabled me to be involved in the commercial decision-making side of the business but ultimately had "no teeth". I began to see myself as always

knocking but not being let in, which led me to question the future and how and where I saw myself in 10 years time. Following a particularly stressful couple of months it all came to a head and I took the plunge and handed in my notice and proceeded to work my 3 months notice. I can honestly say that during that 3 months I never regretted my decision nor have I since.

2. Hardest thing

Starting IS the hardest thing. We all have the idea that it would be good to be your own boss, the question is how and doing what? And once you decide what, you then have to make a business plan and decide are you going to be limited, a sole trader, a partnership? What about VAT? What are you going to call yourself? Everything seems daunting. You know there are numerous routes to go to get the information you need to answer all the questions but just making that first foray into answering all this can be a bridge too far. And it's really scary living that last month of salaried time.

3. Best thing

Realising you can do it and telling people that you run your own business. And yes, proving to those around you that were sceptical about your decision to go it alone. I have discovered that "I told you so" is just as pleasing to say as an adult as it was as a child. I haven't actually said it but thought it many times when witnessing the looks on those doubting Thomas's faces when I answer the *"How's it going?"* question.

4. Biggest mistake

My biggest mistake was underselling myself on my first piece of business – I was warned not to but there you go, it's only money. I haven't made the same mistake since though!

5. Advice
Talk to as many people as you can to discuss your business idea, ask for their advice and thoughts on your proposal. Talk to an accountant early on. And believe that you can, this will help make it happen.

Peter Dann

Business: brand communications research
Employees: 8 plus 3 in joint venture subsidiary
Years: 6

1. What made you start?
I was frustrated by the owner of my current place – they bought the vision of what I wanted to do but wouldn't fund it or give us the independence to fund it ourselves.

2. Hardest thing
The workload, especially the infrastructure (post room and accounts in particular). And the creeping awareness that it was now me alone that my clients were buying, and would they continue to? (This has still not left me!)

3. Best thing
Paying in the first cheque knowing that I could keep rather more of it than before. And the creeping realisation that it was now me alone that my clients were buying. (This has diminished with more partners but still not left me either.)

4. Biggest mistake
Trying to do all the infrastructure myself. Not that big a mistake. We're lucky enough to have avoided anything as dramatic as a disaster (touch wood) but I can give you

some amusing moments, e.g. locking ourselves out of our first office on the day we moved in; accidentally paying myself double and having to give it all back...

5. Advice
Do it. If you build it they will come.

Peter Davies

Business: design and web development
Employees: 11
Years: 13

1. What made you start?
Previous bigger partnership went bust due to recession. Still had good contacts and experience in this area of business.

2. Hardest thing
Cash flow and recruitment.

3. Best thing
Turning my business into a lifestyle business, having flexibility for time for my family.

4. Biggest mistake
Not firing my web director sooner. Went on for two years so took my eye off the ball. Company lost direction and business because of it.

5. Advice
Be very careful who you recruit. Don't go for cheap and cheerful. Go for talent and overpay. Good project management is key as well.

Matthew Durdy

Business: biotechnology
Employees: 5
Years: <1

1. What made you start?
Control and opportunity.

2. Hardest thing
Personal isolation and lack of specialist expertise.

3. Best thing
Being able to do things the way you know is right.

4. Biggest mistake
Failure of part of the technology, and trusting in others to prevent it.

5. Advice
If it doesn't all stack up 100% from a business point of view then it probably isn't right to do it. You need it to be 100% perfect on paper for it to have a chance in reality.

Tim Ellis

Business: song writing and music production
Employees: 1
Years: for ever

1. What made you start?
I'm unemployable.

2. Hardest thing
Diving into the unknown.

3. Best thing
The unknown.

4. Biggest mistake
Starting my own business (only joking… I couldn't do anything else).

5. Advice
Don't start your own business to make money, do it so you can spend every day doing something you love.

Anne Esler

Business: recruitment consultancy
Employees: 12
Business: 10

1. What made you start?
Along with three other partners, I felt that there was a niche for a recruitment consultancy that specialised in providing good quality freelance resource to the marketing services world – people with real talent who had genuinely chosen to work on a flexible freelance/consultancy basis. It was a simple but mould-breaking idea.

2. Hardest thing
Cash flow – making sure that the money came in when we anticipated it would.

3. Best thing
The fact that we succeeded and now we are synonymous with good quality freelancers even though we have expanded the offer and now provide talent on a permanent basis too.

4. Biggest mistake

Numerous! Not putting as much effort or consistent effort behind business development as we should have. Not being as clear as we should have been in the early days about the roles of each of the partners. Not having more dissonance amongst the partners – we tended to agree too much on issues and didn't question each other as much as we should have. Not seeking outside investment early enough to expand the business. Not having better financial support systems internally.

5. Advice

Believe in yourself and your offer and never ever take your foot off the pedal of business development!

Ian Fairbrother

Business: media consultancy
Employees: 35
Years: 17

1. What made you start?
Wanted to work for myself and there was a gap in the market.

2. Hardest thing
Working on my own for three months.

3. Best thing
Freedom.

4. Biggest mistake
Did not exploit European opportunity quickly enough.

5. Advice
Just do it.

Ian Farrow

Business: public relations
Employees: 1
Business: 3

1. What made you start?

I had a burning desire to make all the decisions myself and to create an environment where I could control (to a large extent) where and when to commit my time and efforts. So it was partly lifestyle change and partly the need for control.

2. Hardest thing

I am not a natural optimist. The hardest thing for me was to believe that it would succeed and that I had a saleable commodity.

3. Best thing

Freedom. It is up to me to either fail or succeed. That level of objectivity was not apparent to me when I was employed by others.

4. Biggest mistake

Not treating every job commercially. When you work for a cause for no profit it will quickly eat into billable hours – be careful! Also, my accounts were a bit of a disaster when I started out!

5. Advice

Get an accountant.

Tina Fegent

Business: purchasing consultancy
Employees: 1
Years: 1

1. What made you start?

Having the unique experience of having worked on both the agency and client side, I knew that I could offer a service that would really help both agencies and clients on how to work better together on all purchasing related matters.

2. Hardest thing

Generating the leads and sitting down to think about the network that you have and how you could work with your network to get the sales leads. Also, when you get your first rejection from a potential client, that is hard. You just need to dust yourself down and pick up the phone (Kevin's book *Running Your Own Business*, Chapter 4!).

3. Best thing

The variety of projects. I have really enjoyed all the clients and projects that I have had. Variety is the spice of life and I keep on learning on each project, which makes me a better consultant to future clients.

4. Biggest mistake

Not being aware that sometimes you could be talking or pitching to a new client in a competitive situation. Always know the marketplace and if you are in a "tender" situation.

5. Advice

Really establish who your potential clients are and start to build up your network before you start your own business and keep marketing tools such as your website always up to date.

Marcel Feigel

Nature of business: creative consultancy
Number of employees: 1
Years in business: 20

1. What made you start?
I saw how others were doing the work (including the agency I worked for) and that they were frequently over-complicating it and putting their own agenda on it. I thought I could do a better job. I also thought I was spending a lot of non-productive time in my agency.

2. Hardest thing
The hardest thing I found was establishing credibility and making people aware that you were there; in other words, being taken seriously. I had a couple of clients who I knew well. Building from that was what proved to be difficult.

3. Best thing
The best thing about it is that you can really concentrate on the work and within reason eliminate the politics. You can show what you can do and be judged on what you produce. There are no intermediaries, you forge a much more direct relationship with the client. The more direct the relationship, the greater the chance of work going through undiluted. I also like the fact that when I'm busy I'm busy, and when I'm not I can do other things. I don't have to hang around or pretend.

4. Biggest mistake
My biggest mistake was to trust a client who had a blue chip name who I didn't know particularly well who suddenly went down owing me – and worse, my suppliers – a considerable amount of money. Since then I've been more careful, but trusting clients and knowing how far you can go before confronting them is always a problem, because one bad mistake can literally ruin you. So I always try to keep track of how things are going every step of the way.

5. Advice
I'll give two. Sometimes when a client has really been bad news or more trouble than they're worth, it's best

to say goodbye. This is always difficult, especially when it's a fairly well known company, but it is often the right answer.

The second is to be fully aware of just what you're getting into. Starting a business is always a much more complicated process than anyone imagines. There are a lot of factors to consider that you never thought about. The more you know, the better off you'll be. And if you can take a business course or read one of Kevin's books and really study it, you'll be better off in the long run.

Paul Flynn

Business: music publisher
Employees: 3 (including 2 directors)
Years: 2

1. What made you start?
Our previous employers decided to close their London office but still needed someone to manage the operation and look after their repertoire. We knew the songs, had relationships with the writers and managers, and could do the job for them at a competitive rate while at the same time building our own repertoire.

2. Hardest thing
Because we had been running the previous operation almost as our own before there was no major change in day to day life but the psychological leap from employee to employer took a while to get my head around.

3. Best thing
Knowing that I now have a stake in my own future for better or for worse.

4. Biggest mistake
Thankfully nothing major so far but the worst was trusting someone to come good when all the signs were telling you to move on.

5. Advice
Don't be afraid to go home. Insurmountable problems will frequently appear so much more manageable in the morning. Talk! Don't bottle up problems or grievances. It will only make them worse.

Giles Fraser

Business: public relations
Employees: 50
Years: 7

1. What made you start?
- Wanted more control over my life.
- Thought we could do it better than existing agencies.

2. Hardest thing
Hiring good people.

3. Best thing
Running the business with a great business partner, and seeing lots of people develop into great people.

4. Biggest mistake
Sometimes in the early days we expected senior people to take on more than they were capable of.

5. Advice
Don't be shy to be tough about financial Terms and Conditions and stick to them.

Peter Gaze

Business: funding for companies pre-IPO, investor relations
Employees: 1 (with strong part-time management network)
Years: 5

1. What made you start?
Desire for freedom.

2. Hardest thing
Slow, slow start.

3. Best thing
Almost everything.

4. Biggest mistake
Having a website and putting an advert in the CBI diary – totally pointless.

5. Advice
Network, network, network ... anyone who will listen.

Shelia Gimson

Business: public relations
Employees: 60
Years: 19

1. What made you start?
Four of us working for a consultancy were increasingly dissatisfied with the behaviour of the managing director. He made promises regarding bonuses that were not kept, he spent company money on his own lifestyle, and he was

feeding an alcohol problem – which he didn't admit to at the time. As one of my colleagues said: "This could be a good business, if it wasn't for the Managing Director."

2. Hardest thing
Being cut adrift from a regular and guaranteed salary in the first few months. And working out of someone's flat before we obtained our first office.

3. Best thing
The goodwill of potential clients towards a start up company – they get caught up in the enthusiasm.

4. Biggest mistake
We were joined at the start by the partner of one of the original four colleagues. We only found out years later that each of us believed the others had agreed to this. When things went well this was less of a problem, but it was eventually the major factor in our amicably splitting the company.

5. Advice
Learn the techniques of negotiation, keep an eye on cash flow, and get back up fighting every time you're knocked down.

Laurence Green

Business: advertising
Employees: 100+
Years: 10+

1. What made you start?
Young children to provide for, a sense that business could be done better, and a random moment of opportunism.

2. Hardest thing
Rounding out the team.

3. Best thing
Growing without compromising our launch principles.

4. Biggest mistake
Expending too much time, energy and emotion on tactical new business efforts.

5. Advice
The more you put in, the more you get out.

Steve Greensted

Business: business consultancy
Employees: 3
Years: two-and-a-half

1. What made you start?
I was working in an advertising agency, but had clients who weren't particularly interested in advertising, principally because it was the least of their worries. Most of my time was spent talking to them about non-advertising issues. I'd been working long enough to have sufficient experience to be able to do this credibly. By coincidence, an old boss of mine was in the same position. We both felt that we could make a good living out of helping small and medium companies grow manageably and profitably, and that we had sufficient contacts between the two of us to find some initial clients. Other things had changed which helped us start up. We didn't need offices because mobile phones and Wi-Fi laptops were now both available. And, whereas previously you weren't

taken seriously if you didn't have offices, most of the people we were going to target didn't have any airs and graces.

2. Hardest thing
We didn't have great difficulties in finding customers, but we did have difficulties getting information and data. Our value to our clients is partly based on us knowing things that they don't know, so data is essential. It's also very expensive. However, we eventually found a simple way of getting round this obstacle, but we did greatly miss the information resources that our previous employers had to hand.

3. Best thing
I'm learning new things. I had definitely started to stagnate in advertising.

4. Biggest mistake
We lost a client because we were too greedy.

5. Advice
Don't start on your own. If you're hit by a bus, that's then the end of your business.

Irma Hamilton-Hunt

Business: recruitment
Employees: 35 permanent, 900 temporary
Years: 15

1. What made you start?
I wanted to make a lot of money and know I couldn't do that by working for somebody else.

2. Hardest thing
Trying to keep motivated when I was trying so hard and nothing was happening.

3. Best thing
It would have to be making the company grow and having a great team (I was very proud).

4. Biggest mistake
Can't really think of one.

5. Advice
Enjoy it as life is too short to get to be stressed and after all it's only money!

John Hartley

Business: marketing consulting
Employees: 1–7
Years: 7

1. What made you start?
In the end it's not a choice. It's a compulsion. I'm the only child of two self-employed parents so I grew up with it round the dinner table. I just didn't value corporate jobs. "Real" work meant being self-employed, not being a salary man. That was the apprenticeship – learning a trade.

2. Hardest thing
I don't think starting was hard at all. In a people business, it's just a laptop, a mobile phone and almost zero risk. The first couple of years were a pure adrenaline rush. It was harder to stop working than to start. When the overheads top £1m and you are the sole owner then there

is real and terrifying risk to consider but that comes later. But there is a big difference starting a people business versus anything that involves real capital investment. To me, starting a gastropub would represent a terrifying degree of risk! And people are doing that kind of thing all the time. Starting a people business is a very easy ride by comparison.

3. Best thing
You decide when to stop as well as start. I've just gone solo again (retired?) and my employees have left with thumping tax-free bonuses so they can do exciting things with their lives too. And I can now spend time with my wife and one-year-old as well as improve my guitar playing. Inevitably I'll do stuff on request for longstanding clients and I have a couple of non-exec directorships so I can never be said to have retired completely but it will be a relatively small part of my life.

4. Biggest mistake
We grew very fast with one customer so whilst we made a lot of money quickly, it sapped the desire to promote the business more widely. It's probably better to build steadily to success. A start-up is always susceptible to becoming dependent on one client – so make it a big one!

5. Advice
Think hard about your location. If you want a scaleable business then London lacks any sustainable advantage over Barcelona or Mumbai. If you want to build relationships with blue chip companies, North East USA is the only place to be – a handful of the world's companies operate out of Europe, let alone the UK. And if the UK gets locked in one of its age-old battles with inflation then the currency will be a long-term problem too.

Gordon Haxton

Business: chartered accountants
Employees: 8
Years: 19

1. What made you start?
Being made redundant, after being given a £1,000 thank you by the owners who sold for £60m!

2. Hardest thing
Convincing myself I could do it.

3. Best thing
Not having to answer to someone else, and having great clients.

4. Biggest mistake
Not trusting myself to build a bigger business than the one I have.

5. Advice
Have a plan for 5 years and act upon it. Don't look for negatives.

Tom Helliwell

Nature of business: pubs (2)
Number of employees: around 24. It changes every week, and part of the operation is outsourced
Years in business: 5

1. What made you start?
I wanted to run my own business from the age of 15. I have some narcissistic traits which mean I often believe I know

more than my boss, and often my boss sees me as a threat, so I always used to get fired.

2. Hardest thing
Money. From raising finance to how to pay people, and how to register your own business as a going concern. Unless you know someone that started running their own business there is no one to help you. The government departments that are there to help have got no idea as not one of them has started their own business.

3. Best thing
No one, except my bank balance can make decisions for me. It is my destiny. I work as hard as I want (not as little as I want) and start at what time of day I want and do what I want that day.

4. Biggest mistake
Not doing it 15 years earlier.

5. Advice
Don't listen to the non-believers that are working for "institutions" who tell you "you will fail". If you work hard and focus on most of the right areas you will succeed.

Rassami Hok-Ljungberg

Business: corporate communications
Employees: 2–3
Years: 3+

1. What made you start?
I was asked by some old colleagues and business contacts to help them out with some work, and as I was rather unhappy in the corporate position I was in at the time, I

thought setting up on my own would be a positive and creative way of ensuring I work with people I like and respect, as well as doing the kind of work I enjoy and am good at. Basically, it was taking charge of my own destiny and accepting responsibility for my own personal development and happiness.

2. Hardest thing

Feeling and making others feel that I actually was good, and knew what I was doing. Also getting to grips with "not working for someone else" but being proud of being independent, on my own. Not having a big corporate brand name to hide behind took some time getting used to as it had always been part of my identity. Now it was just me, and people had to buy "just me".

3. Best thing

I work with people and businesses I believe in and like. I am true to myself, my values, and beliefs, and don't have to subscribe to any "corporate lying or spinning". No more corporate clock-watching: I am responsible for my own working time and when I do it. I only answer to myself, but I am also proving to be my hardest boss.

4. Biggest mistake

Not chasing outstanding money when I should have, and not being conscientious about some of the "letter of agreement/contracts" that I should have ensured that I received. If you don't get paid, then don't keep working for a client – unless you are happy to do free work.

5. Advice

Make sure you really want to set up on your own and that you assess what is important for you to make you happy working – and then go about fulfilling those needs in a "non-corporate" way, e.g. creating informal support networks.

Camilla Honey

Business: new business training for communication agencies
Employees: 4
Years: 4

1. What made you start?
To be able to run my life the way I wanted to and create my dream job.

2. Hardest thing
The finances. If I was a student I would have lived off baked beans, but with two start-up businesses in our house and two children to feed it was not so easy – whilst also not wanting to compromise on the quality of our product.

3. Best thing
The satisfaction of creating a business from scratch and seeing it year by year reaching where you want it to.

4. Biggest mistake
Biggest mistake in the early days was not being ruthless enough about time.

5. Advice
Better to do 80% today, than 100% tomorrow. Decide what you want, write a plan then stick to it – JFDI!

Ian Humphreys

Business: marketing
Employees: 10
Years: 7

1. What made you start?

I always had a yearning to be my own boss and was arrogant enough to think I was as good as any one I had ever worked for. But the vital thing that turned a yearning into action was being made redundant. It gave me:

- Motive: (I'll show 'em).
- Desire: I did not want my employment to be at the whim of idiots ever again.
- Opportunity: They made me redundant so my clients were fair game and any contractual ties null and void. And I could always sue for unfair dismissal as the redundancy was not valid with no consultation, notice, etc. Angry? You'd better believe it.

2. Hardest thing

Cash, or the lack of it. Went two months without any remuneration.

3. Best thing

Master of my own destiny. I decide how long I work, who I work for and what I do all day. If it's cocked up it's my fault and if it's great it's down to me – that is empowering. The money reward is also good.

4. Biggest mistake

Employing a new business manager at a time when the business was declining. Pretty soon this extra cost against declining sales forced some harsh decisions and resulted in a restructure of the business. It felt crap making people redundant. Speculative growth spurts should be done from a position of strength otherwise adjust your costs and focus what you are good at. In our case developing our existing network and growth with existing clients.

5. Advice
Make sure you can cover your mortgage, get your family on side and go for it.

Julian Hurst

Business: exhibition and conference organisers/event management
Employees: 5
Years: 5

1. What made you start?
Desire to create something special.

2. Hardest thing
Convincing customers when we had no track record as a company that we were special.

3. Best thing
Seeing the tangible results of doing things better than our competitors.

4. Biggest mistake
12-hour days for far too long.

5. Advice
Get the work/life balance right as soon as possible. I know too many people who have been running businesses for 10 years plus who still work 12-hour days.

Vanella Jackson

Business: research
Employees: 2

1. What made you start?
Desire to live by my own values and beliefs.

2. Hardest thing
Uncertainty and risk.

3. Best thing
Liberation, the thrill of winning the business and having happy clients, the people around you that believe in the same things and are committed to fulfilling the dream.

4. Biggest mistake
Hiring someone who doesn't share the same values and dream.

5. Advice
Be brave.

Christopher Jenkins

Business: accountancy
Employees: 65
Years: 24

1. What made you start?
I like smoking at work (i.e. I am unemployable).

2. Hardest thing
Nothing, it was SO EASY! Then it got difficult. If I had planned it better it would have been the other way round.

3. Best thing
Being the architect of my social environment. I interview everyone and can therefore choose my work colleagues.

4. Biggest mistake
Bringing in external finance with management attached to it. Not looking after No. 1.

5. Advice
Process is all.

Sarah Jennings

Business: communications planning, data management, training
Employees: 3 so far
Years: 2

1. What made you start?
Had always wanted to do it and a combination of right time and opportunity presented itself.

2. Hardest thing
Getting a VAT number and the impact that had on cash flow for the first six months (i.e. no cash flow!).

3. Best thing
Making my own decisions. Seeing those decisions turn into business for the company.

4. Biggest mistake
Nothing major yet but we want to be less reliant on a couple of major accounts and more recession proof. Our biggest missed opportunity was not knowing about flat rate VAT schemes.

5. Advice
Take the time and trouble to really understand your finances and cash flow. People assume you know a lot more than you do.

Cathy Johnson

Business: graphic design
Employees: 4, all part-time
Years: 27

1. What made you start?
Hated my boss!

2. Hardest thing
Working alone.

3. Best thing
Freedom and independence.

4. Biggest mistake
Not trusting my instincts.

5. Advice
Successful people have successful habits.

Daf Jones

Business: session musician
Employees: 1
Years: 10+

1. What made you start?
I saw the potential of turning a great hobby into a reasonable living.

2. Hardest thing
Starting a new venture not only meant moving to a new locality but also there was a huge change in lifestyle. Taking the step from being a successful hobbyist to being a

professional meant having the courage and determination to believe that I could compete successfully at a higher level.

3. Best thing
I earn a living doing what I enjoy most in life. I'm my own boss as far as the jobs I commit to doing, which means I get to work with different people in a variety of different situations and places. It's also great that a large portion of my duties is done from home.

4. Biggest mistake
I was once in a good situation, but I now regret not having searched for something even better during that time. In retrospect, I can see that I didn't keep my options open so as to improve my situation to an even greater extent.

5. Advice
The harder you work the luckier you get. Always give equal time and effort to networking and advertising as well as to developing your products, skills and talents to your maximum potential. Also, be diligent in researching different aspects of your field of trading and expertise. e.g. Set-up costs, opportunities available, competition.

Caroline Kinsey

Business: food and lifestyle public relations
Employees: 14
Business: 9

1. What made you start?
By default! I was working in-house at a major corporation doing a fair amount of travelling missing out on watching my two young daughters grow up, who at the time were 4 and 2. I decided it was easier to work for myself and be

rewarded for all the energy and commitment I have always given to every job I've had.

2. *Hardest thing*

Not knowing where to start! I'd never worked in a PR agency and I'd never run my own business. Everything was a steep learning curve at every level through from deciding the strategic direction for the business down to selecting the right cartridges for the printer.

3. *Best thing*

Both the freedom and sense of pride you feel in what you have created. As a working mother to manage my own timetable whilst juggling various family demands is priceless. Then to build a successful business which now has an impressive reputation and continues to grow at double digit levels every year reinforces the constant sense of achievement I feel. My daughters came to the offices recently and even commented on how proud I must feel about what I've created and I couldn't have asked for higher endorsement than from my children.

4. *Biggest mistake*

Biggest mistake was not to invest in a proper IT infrastructure from the beginning. I chose a cheaper route and hired a one-man band who set me up with my own back-up server. However he suddenly disappeared off the face of the earth and after 60 days my software on the server crashed as he'd only given me trial software. I lost so much key information and spent the next few months cursing the guy. IT is so fundamental within any business that you must employ someone you trust entirely.

5. *Advice*

This would be my advice although I'm not entirely sure I've cracked it myself! Business is getting more and more demanding and it's very easy to slip into the 24/7 culture where you eat, sleep, dream your business. Being able to switch off and relax is just as valuable as putting in those extra hours so that you have renewed energy to tackle the day-to-day freneticism. Fitness has been my antidote to high blood pressure and also offers productive thinking time. Try to step outside from the minutiae of business and keep focused on the bigger picture.

Stephen Knight

Business: marketing
Employees: 1, plus a network of freelance talent
Years: 1

1. What made you start?
Fed up with corporate life and I wanted more flexibility in my working day. Besides, I became unemployable – too many opinions!

2. Hardest thing
I could say finance, finding good people, or knowing what I wanted to do but in truth it was having the confidence to give it a go.

3. Best thing
The flexibility and excitement – every day is different. I have met some great people and had lots of fun doing a huge range of projects – seeing something come together and making a difference to someone's business is hugely rewarding.

4. Biggest mistake
I've been too trusting and naïve – I thought that everyone had the same agenda and outlook and have been sadly mistaken albeit only on a handful of occasions.

5. Advice
Work hard – put in the hours, enjoy what you do – never become complacent. Develop a positive mindset and outlook and look for the best in people but guard against becoming too dependent on one client or one supplier – be prepared to change your plan constantly and take advantage of new opportunities when they happen. Accept that it won't always work but learn as you go along and be prepared to take calculated risks.

Peter Law

Business: public relations, and have since acquired a research business
Employees: 16
Years in business: 14 (second business, first one sold)

1. What made you start?
Wanted to take control of own destiny and create a working/living culture/environment based on a set of core beliefs and values; belief in own talent; desire to make more money; belief that I/we could offer something more valuable/effective to the marketplace than others.

2. Hardest thing
Never enjoyed the nuts and bolts of office logistics, so finding office and equipping it was the hardest.

3. Best thing
Building a business based on empowering people, which delivers for everyone involved: clients, staff, me and my family, and most recently shareholders.

4. Biggest mistake
Being too busy/content/short-sighted not to take the trouble to try to get on the government roster just before our then core market of media, telecommunications and IT began to shrink after the dotcom bubble burst, and government/ public sector work started to boom.

5. Advice
Get a good business coach on day one and set your goals for the next 5 years, starting with year 5 and working backwards (the 5–3–1 plan). I discovered coaching when things started to get tough and it saved me and the business. I wish I'd known about it sooner. In fact, the experience was so positive that once we were back on track, I took time out to train as a business coach and proceeded to coach my own business through three years of almost 100% fee income growth and a stock market flotation. I continue using coaching as an important tool in next stage of growth, and also coach other businesses and business leaders.

Stephen Martin

Business: customer analyst
Employees: 3–10
Years: 4

1. What made you start?
Three things came together:

- The sales leads from the parent company dried up and I believed that I could do better myself.
- There was nothing about the parent company that I enjoyed.

- A flexible mortgage gave me access to 3 times as much money as my notice period so I had a safety net.

2. Hardest thing
Self-belief and the confidence to hire someone.

3. Best thing
Self-determination and the capacity to earn more by working harder.

4. Biggest mistake
Biggest mistake is slacking off on the selling and networking when I am busy. Worst disaster is when a client's MD got fired and all the expected income went up in the air – at a time when they were the only customer!

5. Advice
There seems to be a Catch 22 to resolve. Businesses that have value so that you can sell them need investment, which makes the business more risky and more likely to fail.

Zena Martin

Business: diversity communications consulting
Employees: 1, plus 10 independent consultants
Years: 2

1. What made you start?
I have always been fairly entrepreneurial and a risk-taker. I could also see that the UK would follow the US in terms of targeting diverse audiences. I approached my then parent company, who did not embrace the idea, although it has

had a Diversity Division in the US since 1987, so I decided to set up the business myself.

2. Hardest thing
Giving up my six-figure salary and the resources of a global media group to get work done.

3. Best thing
Being able to dictate my own schedule, still live where I've been living for the last 5 years, spend more time doing charity work and being a non-exec director, work with the most amazingly varied client portfolio of very big names, and now, knowing that my gut was absolutely, positively right.

4. Biggest mistake
Considering letting a larger company that approached me buy my company, when it was way too early to talk about it.

5. Advice
Never expect your clients to pay you on time.

Simon Mathews

Business: brand & communication strategy
Employees: 8 – only employ senior people
Years: 4

1. What made you start?
My interest in developing a better way of working and a complete lack of faith in the listed agency groups to evolve a new agency model or process in a changing communication world.

2. Hardest thing
Selling in a new way of working to a risk-averse client community.

3. Best thing
Getting to the point in our growth and work where we can prove to clients that it's worth taking that risk, e.g. case studies.

4. Biggest mistake
Not being more careful about selecting my start up partners and making really sure that they wanted to go through the pain of building their own vision of a business… neither of them worked out and had to be replaced! It probably set us back by at least a year.

5. Advice
Do it because you love it, not for the perceived money (that may come in time BUT only if you love it).

Chris Matthews

Business: financial & corporate public relations
Employees: 24
Years: 10

1. What made you start?
It was a sense of frustration with my previous employer, coupled with a belief that there was a better way to do things, that made me decide to start the business.

2. Hardest thing
Just doing it. We have all met people who are going to start their own business "one day", but who never ever get around to it. You can do all the planning and research you

want (and you should invest time in this), but there comes a moment when you have to take a deep breath and get going. Sure, it involves risk. Yes, it involves cost. Yup, it could all go wrong. But if you don't stop dreaming and start doing, you will never know what you might achieve. As the ad says: "Just do it."

3. Best thing
The best thing has been being part of something that's growing and growing. We had one client when we started out. We now have about sixty retained and about twenty project clients at any one time and regularly feature in the top ten league tables for our industry. That and watching the folk in the company develop – that's immensely satisfying.

4. Biggest mistake
Losing a large client – that was truly awful. It didn't dent our growth (we have had unbroken growth for the last ten years) but it reminded us, very, very painfully, that you have to keep working at success, each and every day. Were they right to fire us; had we done wrong? No – we were doing a cracking job, but a new client executive wanted to work with a team familiar to them and so we were out. That happens – but it still hurt.

5. Advice
Get a mentor. Our Chairman has been through it before and his advice and counsel is invaluable. A second piece of advice – keep the business fresh; new thinking, new faces, stay on top of the trends.

Mark McCallum

Business: writer
Employees: 1

1. What made you start?

The need to change my life, get out of a rut and see if I could use my brain for my own benefit rather than others.

2. Hardest thing

Overcoming the uncertainty, developing a tougher skin and being prepared to initiate new business when, within a company, business came to me.

3. Best thing

Making interesting connections with people with whom I now work – a kind of virtuous circle of associates. Having the freedom to diversify and take on projects that I'd never have expected to work on within the strictures of company life.

4. Biggest mistake

I'd have to answer that with my biggest failing, which would be not to remorselessly pursue every idea within the parameters of what I do, as opposed to blindly following a lead just for the sake of it.

5. Advice

Learn to appreciate that what you know is valuable. Just because you take it for granted doesn't mean it is commonplace knowledge. Know your strengths and compensate fully for your weaknesses. Get a good accountant. Get something produced/commissioned/done. A finished project says a lot more about you than the possibility of one.

Peter McCamley

Business: music publisher
Employees: 3 (including 2 directors)
Years: 2

1. What made you start?
I was made redundant by my previous firm. Having been an employee for over 22 years I realised that unless I had my own business this could happen again.

2. Hardest thing
Finance. I was lucky to be in a position where I could start a business and just about cover my overheads from day one.

3. Best thing
Many things. In my business it's all about owning assets. We have managed to acquire valuable assets, which have given our business (less than 2 years old) a value.

4. Biggest mistake
So far (fingers crossed) we have not experienced any downside.

5. Advice
Have belief in yourself.

Manisha Mehta

Business: ethical clothing
Employees: 3 and a number of interns
Years: less than 2

1. What made you start?
Desire to do something good and take more control of my life. The challenge of creating something that big!

2. Hardest thing
I actually didn't find it hard to get started. Things, more or less, fell into place.

3. Best thing
Knowing that I can do it.

4. Biggest mistake
Rushing the business too much: trying to get started on too large a scale and not knowing my business partner well enough.

5. Advice
To start on a smaller scale to get a real idea of the market, field, etc. so that mistakes can happen on a smaller, more manageable scale. Also, that you will always need more money than your worst forecasts!

Juan Montes

Business: company advisor in digital content and media
Employees: 1
Years: 3

1. What made you start?
Wanting to diversify from a single company with its own market and objectives to make my experience available across a wider set of companies with their own challenges and problems to solve. Much more instant feeling of satisfaction on the use of previously acquired skill set.

2. Hardest thing
Getting the balance right between carrying out work for the business and developing new future prospects to ensure there is an even spread of work.

3. Best thing
The feeling of making a contribution in a short time to different customers.

4. Biggest mistake
Don't know yet.

5. Advice
Always be willing to help potential customers and colleagues with your knowledge without becoming too commercial at too early a stage. In case of doubt be generous – it will sustain you in the long run.

Adam Morgan

Business: marketing consultancy
Employees: 12
Years: 8

1. What made you start?
Wrote a book for my advertising agency, and when I finished it 18 months later they said they didn't want it any more, and that it was not a basis for a positioning. So, driven by anger and bile, I decided to leave and show them there was.

2. Hardest thing
Finding good people to work alongside you.

3. Best thing
Freedom. No one looking over my shoulder and telling me what to do.

4. Biggest mistake
Almost burning out. Not looking after myself and my personal relationship enough in one critical business year.

5. Advice
I thought that success in this business was all about great content. Content is important, but I only realized three years in that it is really all about the relationship. Nurturing and keeping the key relationships healthy is the most important aspect of my job.

Ivan Mulcahy

Business: literary agency
Employees: 5
Years: 4

1. What made you start?
I was utterly bored with my previous career and couldn't motivate myself any more, despite having been successful in previous years.

2. Hardest thing
Finding a business partner that I could trust, who was hard working and competent.

3. Best thing
Doing exactly what I wanted to do.

4. Biggest mistake
Underestimating the investment level needed to get it going in the first three years.

5. Advice
Be really sure about the people you choose to work with. It's emotionally intense and highly stressful and you need to be doing it with people you like, trust and respect.

Mo Murphy

Business: public relations
Employees: 1 (subcontract to network of others when required)
Years: 6

1. What made you start?
I was pregnant and wanted something that would be more flexible around family life and be less depressing and more honest than the corporate environment I'd just left. If I worked for myself I thought I'd be better able to "tick those boxes".

2. Hardest thing
I feel there was nothing hard about starting – I enjoyed it all and found it all really exciting (maybe that was more to do with knowing I was starting a HUGE new chapter of my life with a baby on the way too) – I was lucky that I had some great contacts who wanted to work with me right from the start so it didn't feel as scary maybe as starting from a total zero client list. The hardest thing for me was later – juggling a baby and work (it isn't easy!). Times when maybe cash flow isn't so great and having to chase payment or when I miss the creative collaboration with other colleagues.

3. Best thing
Such a cliché – but being my own boss and No Politics!! I get to concentrate on the real stuff – client work and don't have to worry about all the petty admin stuff I HAD to do in my previous agency. Some of the "professional practices" and the way we charged clients I felt was somewhat questionable and I'm happy to be out of that. I'm also glad not to be responsible for the career direction of an entire team of go-getting 20-somethings, and not having dreadful profit and loss meetings with an accountant every Monday morning – that has to be good!

4. Biggest mistake
Well I wouldn't call it a disaster – but it's been my biggest mistake so far – was working for a US client who asked me to

commit to an exchange rate range for my work (so I agreed to bill in pounds but they would only pay me that rate IF the dollar was between X and Y to the pound) – and the US dollar then promptly tanked so I lost several thousand pounds in the currency translation – and the best thing about that is I learnt not to do it again with my next American client!

5. Advice
Financial planning is key to happy self-employment. Remember that 40% of your fees still belongs to the tax man. So put it in a bank account away from your day-to-day spending.

Don't think you can work off the kitchen table! For me making sure I have a separate office that I can close the door on so I'm not tempted to work more hours than I have to helps keep that work life balance I craved in the first place.

Accept that working for yourself is different. Some weeks maybe I work 7 days a week (which I know sort of contradicts myself) – but that allows me to take time out at other times to enjoy things that maybe if I wasn't self-employed I'd have to pass by. What keeps me self-employed is loving the flexibility of work.

Griselda Mussett

Business: network of businesses in events, archiving website, weekly newsletter
Employees: 1
Years: 4

1. What made you start?
Need, challenge and opportunity. I needed to earn money from home because of family responsibilities. I live in a

rural area, and my skills as a broadcaster are not much in demand. I also wanted to see if I could create a business literally "from thin air".

It was clear to me that with the Internet, everything was changing. Many traditional business expenses could be completely avoided, e.g. specialised and expensive office space, and postal charges. I also thought there must be many people like me trying to start or run a business from home, very isolated and having to master skills and tasks which were not their speciality. Getting everyone together to share experience and give each other work seemed like a good idea.

2. Hardest thing

Pricing. I was far too flippant about the business plan side of things. I read various helpful information from Business Link and the banks but I was not realistic about what I needed to earn. I was partly relying on my husband's support and I think if I had not had this I would have been more hard-nosed. In fact I did not take my idea or myself seriously enough. I started too cheaply, then had to put the price up, which in fact worked out okay, but I should have got this right to start with. I should also have had a bigger vision for my business and not been scared about it growing larger, faster.

3. Best thing

I have loved the positive side of the business – the creative side of it – thinking up my business name, getting the people together at events, designing logo and stationery, helping people with ideas I've picked up or being able to put people in touch. I know my customers like my services (because they tell me!) and it was wonderful when two people approached me out of the blue to ask if they could franchise the operation in their area.

4. Biggest mistake

Two things. First, the website caused a lot of delay and headaches. I tried and failed with four different suppliers. At that time (2003) it was really hard to find affordable professional designers: one eventually admitted he was a long-distance lorry driver who did coding more or less as a hobby. The next team were two college graduates who were great at design but were defeated by my need for a database in the site. Another company who assured me they could do it were in reality two secondary school teachers working part-time in the evenings. All this caused months of delay and wasted money. Things are much better now, both in terms of price and competence.

The second mistake was to employ a rather expensive business consultant to help with pricing and other disciplines. She was helpful but also very dominant and I found it hard to get rid of her. That was a costly error.

5. Advice

Get involved with business organisations and training courses (which are pretty well free or nearly so) not just for the learning opportunities but for the excellent networking and support you get from the other members. You can learn from their mistakes, hear their ideas and innovations, and look for customers among them. Also, read Kevin's books! They are funny and wise.

Michael Pagan

Business: IT consultancy
Employees: 1
Years: 4

1. What made you start?

I started due to redundancy but had been planning my own venture for a while beforehand. This gave me the incentive, time and financial cushion to go out on my own.

2. Hardest thing

a. The revelation that the phone didn't immediately ring with people recognizing my genius without me having to tell them!

b. The sheer length of time it takes between approaching clients and getting money in the bank.

c. Lack of others off whom to bounce ideas.

3. Best thing

Freedom to do other stuff. E.g. write a business book, get involved with my local theatre. Meeting people I wouldn't have met otherwise.

4. Biggest mistake

Biggest mistake was probably sticking too long with an idea that wasn't working. Set a deadline by which time if your idea hasn't worked, overhaul it completely and don't be afraid to kill it off.

5. Advice

Get out more and meet people.

Graham Rittener

Business: recruitment
Employees: 3 partners
Years: 6 months

1. What made you start?

I have always wanted to run my own business. Part of it is a creative urge –wanting to create something from nothing and the satisfaction that gives. Part of it is the notion of wanting to be able to do things my way and not be accountable to anyone, and part of it is for financial reasons, knowing that I could probably do a lot better for myself than having a career all my life. Finally, we spotted a gap in the market, which we thought we could make a success out of.

2. Hardest thing

I started without any grant, loan or capital investment – we used all our own money to set up – therefore, the hardest thing has been the financial pressure.

3. Best thing

The excitement of getting it together, the satisfaction of seeing it work, and the power to orchestrate things the way we want to.

4. Biggest mistake

Our biggest mistake was not getting more working capital to start the company.

5. Advice

Be very focused and be very conservative in your forecasts. Make sure you have enough capital in place to cover your most conservative financial forecasts.

Ben Robbins

Business: music production/song writing/recording studio/ label/artiste management
Employees: 2 directors, 2 staff – rapidly shrinking!
Years: 2

1. What made you start?

The naïve notion that the financial reward would be greater. Obviously the thought of being your own boss is always going to be attractive...

2. Hardest thing

Cash flow.

3. Best thing

Having a wonderful studio to work in with all the toys I could want, and driving a silly car.

4. Biggest mistake

Severe lack of communication with business partner/staff. Letting an "artistic attitude" get in the way of a gritty business like approach – spending beyond our means. Sir Alan Sugar would have a heart attack if he was a fly on our wall!

5. Advice

COMMUNICATION. COMMUNICATION. COMMUNICATION. Leave ego and pride at home please. No room for this in the office AT ALL.

Julian Saunders

Business: marketing consultancy
Employees: 1
Years: 3

1. What made you start?

What motivated me to start my own business was a desire for freedom from corporate life, prompted by the truly loathsome experience of working under my previous boss. It confirmed what I already knew in my heart of hearts. I could not put up with all the nonsense of big ad agencies any more. I had grown out of it.

2. Hardest thing
Getting clients and therefore enough income.

3. Best thing
Waking up and feeling "Right I have got to get on with it. I am only answerable to me". Liberation. And getting used to the ups and downs. You never quite get used to the downs but you learn to accept them. Stuff that you think is going to happen doesn't and things that you were not expecting jump up and surprise you. So you never quite know where you are going to end up next month. It could be Rio or Slough or both.

4. Biggest mistake
I set up the business with someone with whom I was incompatible. He also had his own business so he did not give it 100%. It caused friction. We had to negotiate an amicable separation, which we achieved without rancour.

5. Advice
Make sure that you start up with the right person/people. You are going to be spending a lot of time together. The relationship(s) either gives you energy and stimulation or it saps it. Everything else follows.

Andrew Sawkins

Business: market research
Years: 9
Employees: 6

1. What made you start?

Honestly, I disliked working for someone else. I wanted to make the decisions – right or wrong. Be master of my own destiny.

2. Hardest thing

More an emotional issue than anything else. A worry that clients wouldn't come with me – lack of self-belief I suppose.

3. Best thing

Seeing the work come in. Doubling our expected turnover in the first year.

4. Biggest mistake

Not being prepared for all the work. Thinking we could survive on four people when in fact we should have employed another three. Consequently everyone was overworked, stressed and threatened to leave!

5. Advice

If you want to be your own boss, just do it. Don't spend years debating the pros and cons. Have faith in yourself. If it all goes wrong you can always go back to working for someone else.

Paul Simons

Business: numerous communications agencies and groups
Employees: 1–600
Years: 30+

1. What made you start?

In truth, a combination of fear and ambition. The fear was becoming a highly paid 40 something with my life held in someone else's hands, on a whim. Very scary. On the ambition front, I believed there was a better way!

2. Hardest thing

Probably the agony of the team. I made a pact to start an agency over a long lunch in Soho (what a cliché!). We then convinced others it would be a good idea. The search for the creative partners was hard work. It was very trying and concerning because most were so into themselves and totally inept on the commercial realities of starting a business. Personally I strongly believe the team was the big challenge, everything else is more mechanical.

3. Best thing

The white knuckle rollercoaster ride. It kicked off with a pitch for a large financial services client. We were on the back foot for a long time running to catch up with events out of our control. We won another big account before we had an office. The client agreed a fee, which paid for our first year. We pitched for Nike in an office we didn't actually own at the time, and we won it. The issues just grew exponentially and we just ran as fast as we could to keep up. The margin between success and failure was a weekly subject of partners meetings. It never changed.

4. Biggest mistake

It has to be money. The trap everyone confronts. We were always under capitalised, which means we were driven by cash flow. Most people in advertising don't understand money. Busy = good. Wrong. Busy fools go down the drain. It's a massive topic.

My biggest disaster, headed off at the pass at the 11th hour, was moving in to a new building, lots of money being spent, a stall in the finance process due to the move, then discovering we had bills to pay and no money. We couldn't cover the payroll needed in 2 weeks. We sorted it with cooperation from our bank and we recovered quite quickly but it left an indelible mark on my brain – it remains today.

5. Advice
Campaign (the advertising trade magazine) described us as having "an enviable blend of business brains and creative excellence". I could have married the journalist who wrote this, male or female, as it has to be the ultimate accolade. That's my advice – strive to marry quality delivery with prudent business management, it's a winning formula very few manage to achieve. Stand for something, do it, have the confidence to walk away from things that dilute belief yet have a tough attitude to business considerations.

Cautionary tale
A few years after selling, I joined one of the global networks. A combination of flattery, persistence and the queen's shilling persuaded me to accept a place on the worldwide board and the top job in the UK, the second biggest office in the world after New York. Without doubt it gave me new experiences that have proved to be invaluable and I gave a much-needed injection of spirit and drive to a lacklustre group of around 1200 people.

Over the next two years the London group was the best performer in terms of revenue and profit growth but the tension between my history as an independent business owner versus a player in a global network created strains that became very difficult for all parties. I believe that anyone who has created their own business successfully becomes unemployable.

It is very hard to subjugate beliefs. Passion drives entrepreneurs, so attempting to balance corporate needs with what a person believes is the right course becomes a tug of war – do I keep quiet and take the money or say what I think?

In the end, after two-and-a-half years it all ended in tears and lawyers and pistols at dawn. I was ejected like an organ graft that was rejected by the body – all very messy. It taught me a very important lesson. Bill Bernbach, an icon in the advertising world, once said; "If you stand for something you have people for you and people against you, if you stand for nothing you have neither." So I went back to the basics, started all over again and created a business around my beliefs.

Paul Speers

Business: commercial company doctors
Employees: 4
Years: 2

1. What made you start?
Opportunities that came my way.

2. Hardest thing
Avoiding tax.

3. Best thing
Keeps you on the edge and fresh.

4. Biggest mistake
Thinking I was in finance in a Venture Capitalist meeting.

5. Advice
Don't dream about it, just get on with it – procrastination is a killer.

Sarah Taylor

Business: marketing consultancy, luxury goods
Employees: just me
Years: 18 months

1. What made you start?
Working for myself allows me to do things "my way" and not answer to people I don't respect. It gives me the freedom to work on a range of different projects and not be tied to one area. Nobody "owns me" from 9–5.30pm.

2. Hardest thing
Taking the leap of faith and waving goodbye to the monthly pay cheque!

3. Best thing
Freedom, flexibility and invoices being paid on time.

4. Biggest mistake
Under-pricing and over-delivering – it takes a while to get the balance right.

5. Advice
Really think about your pricing. Recognise that it takes time to build your reputation and business, but don't start too low. Equally, don't price yourself out of the market before you even start. Value what you do (or what you are producing) and maintain your pride and integrity. Oh, and find a good mentor!

Andy Tilley

Business: media strategy consultancy
Employees: 10
Years: 5

1. What made you start?
Reaching forty, being totally frustrated by the way my employer treated our discipline, ignored counsel and refused to change the structure of the business to adapt to the new landscape. At the same time hearing a story from a close friend who had attended Harvard. During a series of interviews with 75 men over 75, almost 80% said they wished they had taken more risks.... Had to do it particularly as a number of my clients suggested it and said they would support it.

2. Hardest thing
Agreeing on a name for the company, which we saw as critical, and which in the end was what it was because it became imbued with the values that we delivered for it. It doesn't matter really so long as it isn't too stupid!

3. Best thing
Having the ability to determine our own destiny and create something unique from scratch.

4. Biggest mistake
Not taking more risks and getting comfortable (see 1. above).

5. Advice
Commercial Darwinism is a continual requirement so take some risks and don't polish turds. Too much time is spent trying to get things perfect when you need to try them out in imperfect form.

David Turner

Business: consumer brand identity design
Employees: 30
Years: 15

1. What made you start?
My Dad had done it and preached its benefits. Also, I always liked making my own decisions.

2. Hardest thing
I'm a lousy networker.

3. Best thing
The feeling of self-determination.

4. Biggest mistake
Not taking more risks. It makes for slow progress.

5. Advice
Avoid eponymous naming. (It's great when you start, but restrictive when you grow. This was the one piece of advice my old boss gave me, and of course, I ignored it.)

Richard Wyatt-Haines

Business: management consultancy
Employees: 15
Years: 8

1. What made you start?
The need for variety, a restless mind, a passionate belief that I could make it on my own and I wanted to test it.

2. Hardest thing
Making the jump from secured income – an unnecessary worry in reality.

3. Best thing
The variety, the buzz, the self-control, the competition.

4. Biggest mistake
Allowing wives of directors to influence company decision-making.

5. Advice
Do it, be very focused, be different from the big players (play to your strength of being small), let others feel your passion – they will buy into it.

Appendix III: Bibliography

Buzz, Salzman, Matathia & O'Reilly (John Wiley, 2003)

Economist Guide to Management Ideas, Tim Hindle (*Economist,* 2003)

Getting Things Done, David Allen (Piatkus, 2001)

Hello Laziness, Corinne Maier (Orion, 2004)

How To Be A Complete And Utter Failure In Life, Work and Everything, Steve McDermott (Pearson, 2002)

How Not To Come Second, David Kean (Marshall Cavendish, 2006)

Juicing The Orange, Pat Fallon and Fred Senn (Harvard Business School Publishing, 2006)

Liar's Paradise, Graham Edmonds (Southbank, 2006)

Screw It, Let's Do It, Richard Branson (Virgin, 2006)

See, Feel, Think, Do, Milligan & Smith (Marshall Cavendish, 2006)

Simply Brilliant, Fergus O'Connell (Prentice Hall, 2001)

So What?, Kevin Duncan (Capstone, 2007)

Teach Yourself Growing Your Business, Kevin Duncan (Hodder & Stoughton, 2006)

Teach Yourself Running Your Own Business, Kevin Duncan (Hodder & Stoughton, 2005)

The Entrepreneur's Book Of Checklists, Robert Ashton (Pearson, 2004)

Index